Using Technology to Support High-Impact Educational Practice

USING TECHNOLOGY TO SUPPORT HIGH-IMPACT EDUCATIONAL PRACTICE

Karen S. Ivers

LIBRARIES
UNLIMITED™
An Imprint of ABC-CLIO, LLC
Santa Barbara, California • Denver, Colorado

Library of Congress Cataloging-in-Publication Data

Names: Ivers, Karen S., author
Title: Using technology to support high-impact educational practice / Karen S. Ivers.
Description: Santa Barbara, California : Libraries Unlimited, an Imprint of ABC-CLIO, LLC, [2019] | Includes bibliographical references and index.
Identifiers: LCCN 2018037768 (print) | LCCN 2018051526 (ebook) | ISBN 9781440867026 (Ebook) | ISBN 9781440867019 (hard copy : alk. paper)
Subjects: LCSH: Educational technology. | Computer-assisted instruction.
Classification: LCC LB1028.3 (ebook) | LCC LB1028.3 .I93 2019 (print) | DDC 371.33–dc23
LC record available at https://lccn.loc.gov/2018037768

ISBN: 978–1–4408–6701–9 (paperback)
   978–1–4408–6702–6 (eBook)

23 22 21 20 19   1 2 3 4 5

This book is also available as an eBook.

Libraries Unlimited
An Imprint of ABC-CLIO, LLC

ABC-CLIO, LLC
130 Cremona Drive, P.O. Box 1911
Santa Barbara, California 93116-1911
www.abc-clio.com

This book is printed on acid-free paper ∞

Manufactured in the United States of America

Contents

Preface vii

Chapter 1: High-Impact Educational Practices 1
    Overview 1
    Outcomes and High-Impact Educational Practices 1
    The Framework for 21st Century Learning 3
    HIP Technology 6
    Preparing Our Students for the Future 9
    Technology Standards and Frameworks 9
    Summary 11
    Activities 12
    Resource List 13
    References 13

Chapter 2: Collaborative Assignments and Projects 19
    Overview 19
    Designing and Managing Small Group Instruction 19
    Designing and Managing Collaborative Activities, Including
    Cooperative Learning 22
    Summary 35
    Activities 35
    Resource List 36
    References 38

**Chapter 3: Social Competence, Culturally Responsive Teaching,
    and Inclusive Classrooms** 49
    Overview 49
    Social Competence 49
    Culturally Responsive Teaching 51
    Just, Equitable, and Inclusive Education 60
    Summary 68
    Activities 69
    Resource List 70
    References 73

Chapter 4: Global Competence 85
    Overview 85
    Global Competence 85
    Summary 100
    Activities 100
    Resource List 102
    References 105

Chapter 5: Service-Learning and Project-Based Learning 109

Overview 109

Service-Learning 109

Project-Based Learning 113

Summary 119

Activities 119

Resource List 120

References 121

Chapter 6: Research, Writing, and Information, Media, and

Technology Skills 129

Overview 129

Research 129

Writing 132

Information, Media, and Information and Communication

Technologies Literacy 136

ePortfolios 142

Digital Citizenship 144

Summary 145

Activities 145

Resource List 147

References 149

Index 155

Preface

Over the past several years, there has been a shift in educational practices at both college and K–12 levels. The advancement, accessibility, and increased integration of technology have created new delivery methods of instruction and learning; social media has magnified everyday communication and how we address global issues in the classroom; and there is an increased awareness of and demand for just, equitable, and inclusive education. High-impact educational practices are beneficial for students from different backgrounds, especially students from underserved populations. Higher institutions of education are incorporating high-impact educational practices to increase student retention and engagement, and K–12 schools are using similar practices to place more emphasis on responsive teaching, critical thinking, creativity, communication, and collaboration.

Using Technology to Support High-Impact Educational Practice emphasizes the importance of good teaching and preparing students for our global and technology-based workforce, noting that technology will continue to evolve and change at a rapid pace. The intent of the book is to focus on the importance of high-impact educational practices (instructional approaches that can increase student retention and engagement) and how technology can be used to support these practices. The book is designed for K–12 credential and master's students and their administrators and faculty, as well as media and information specialists who work with teachers.

Using Technology to Support High-Impact Educational Practice is organized into six chapters. Chapter 1 provides the reader with an overview and research related to high-impact educational practices, 21st-century learning, educational technology standards, and preparing students for the future. Chapters 2 through 6 focus on specific high-impact educational practices and include how technology can support these practices. Each chapter includes activities that allow readers to reflect upon and apply what they have learned. The activities can be conducted face-to-face or online, using discussion forums and other online collaborative learning tools. A list of technology resources is available at the end of each chapter, also. Chapters include High-Impact Educational Practices; Collaborative Assignments and Projects; Social Competence, Culturally Responsive Teaching, and Inclusive Classrooms; Global Competence; Service-Learning and Project-Based Learning; and Research, Writing, and Information, Media, and Technology Skills.

Using Technology to Support High-Impact Educational Practice provides educators with an understanding of the importance of using high-impact educational practices to support students' academic achievement, social and global competence, and success in our diverse, digital 21st-century global community and workforce. Emphasis is placed on critical thinking, communication, collaboration, and creativity; creating just, equitable, and inclusive classroom environments; and providing educators with instructional strategies and technology resources that can be used to support high-impact educational practices in their classrooms.

Chapter 1

High-Impact Educational Practices

OVERVIEW

Over the past several years, there has been a shift in educational practices at both college and K–12 levels. The advancement, accessibility, and increased integration of technology have created new delivery methods of instruction and learning; social media has magnified everyday communication and how we address global issues in the classroom; and there is an increased awareness of and demand for just, equitable, and inclusive education. Higher institutions of education are incorporating *high-impact educational practices*, instructional approaches that can increase student retention and engagement. High-impact educational practices are beneficial for students from different backgrounds, especially students from underserved populations (Kuh 2008). K–12 schools are focusing on just, equitable, and inclusive education, placing more emphasis on responsive teaching, critical thinking, creativity, communication, and collaboration. K–12 schools are engaging students in science, technology, engineering, and math (STEM), also, to prepare students for the 21st-century workforce. K–12 technology standards and frameworks have been written to help educators prepare their students for the demands of the 21st century.

This chapter examines high-impact educational practices and how these practices are beneficial at the K–12 level. The chapter begins by discussing higher education learning outcomes, high-impact educational practices, and how high-impact educational practices align with different outcomes, including the *Framework for 21st Century Learning* (Partnership for 21st Century Skills 2007), a framework designed to help prepare K–12 students to be successful in the 21st-century global community. Next, high-impact practices using technology—HIP technology—are introduced with research supporting the use of high-impact educational practices with K–12 students. Preparing students for the future is discussed. Topics include the significance of technology in today's society, Kelly's (2016) inevitable technology forces, and standards and frameworks for using technology. The chapter concludes with activities that reinforce and extend what was presented in the chapter.

OUTCOMES AND HIGH-IMPACT EDUCATIONAL PRACTICES

In 2005, the Association of American Colleges & Universities (AAC&U) established the Liberal Education and America's Promise (LEAP), a national initiative designed to align college learning outcomes with the needs of the 21st-century global community and workforce. After extensive discussions with faculty and employers, LEAP created a set of essential learning outcomes designed to enable students to succeed and contribute in our ever-changing, global, 21st-century society. Focusing on intellectual and practical skills, broad knowledge, integrative learning, and personal and social responsibility, the Essential Learning Outcomes (Kuh 2008, 4) were designed to help students gain the following:

- **Knowledge of Human Cultures and the Physical and Natural World**

  - Through study in the sciences and mathematics, social sciences, humanities, histories, languages, and the arts
    Focused by engagement with big questions, both contemporary and enduring

- **Intellectual and Practical Skills, including**

  - Inquiry and analysis

  - Critical and creative thinking

  - Written and oral communication

  - Quantitative literacy

  - Information literacy

  - Teamwork and problem solving
    Practiced extensively, across the curriculum, in the context of progressively more challenging problems, projects, and standards for performance

- **Personal and Social Responsibility, including**

  - Civic knowledge and engagement—local and global

  - Intercultural knowledge and competence

  - Ethical reasoning and action

  - Foundations and skills for lifelong learning
    Anchored through active involvement with diverse communities and real-world challenges

- **Integrative and Applied Learning, including**

  - Synthesis and advanced accomplishment across general and specialized studies
    Demonstrated through the application of knowledge, skills, and responsibilities to new settings and complex problems

Excerpted with permission from *College Learning for the New Global Century*. Copyright 2007 by the Association of American Colleges & Universities.

In addition to helping students prepare for the demands of the 21st century, the Essential Learning Outcomes were designed to make excellence inclusive, meaning "setting empowering educational goals for all students and not just some of them" (Kuh 2008, 3).

After establishing outcomes, educators need to consider how they can help all students reach these outcomes meaningfully and successfully. Research suggests that there is a set of educational practices that have proven successful for students from widely varying backgrounds. These are considered *high-impact educational practices* and include small group learning with faculty or staff, common intellectual experiences, learning communities, collaborative assignments and projects, student research, global learning, service-learning and community-based learning, internships, ePortfolios, and capstone or culminating experiences (Kuh 2008; Watson, Kuh, Rhodes, Light, and Chen 2016). According to Kuh (2008), high-impact educational practices include practices that emphasize collaborative learning, critical inquiry, information literacy, frequent writing, and other skills that develop students' intellectual competencies and real-world learning. Findings suggest that high-impact educational practices positively affect student learning, including their critical-thinking skills, intercultural effectiveness, and engagement (Bonet and Walters 2016; BrckaLorenz, Garvey, Hurtado, and Latopolski 2017; Kilgo, Ezell Sheets, and Pascarella 2015). In addition, high-impact educational practices have been shown to increase student retention and provide students with career-related advantages (Bonet and Walters 2016; Miller, Rocconi, and Dumford 2017). Kuh (2008) and Watson, Kuh, Rhodes, Light, and Chen (2016) discuss how high-impact educational practices can support the Essential Learning Outcomes. Table 1.1 shows how high-impact educational practices can support the Essential Learning Outcomes (Kuh 2008; Watson, Kuh, Rhodes, Light, and Chen 2016).

Kuh (2008, 2) notes that "the development of intellectual powers and capacities; ethical and civic preparation; personal growth and self-direction" are fundamental and necessary elements in an excellent education. Other elements change with time, depending on the needs and circumstances of the changing world.

THE FRAMEWORK FOR 21ST CENTURY LEARNING

Similar to the AAC&U's goal of ensuring college students are able to succeed and contribute in today's global society, the Partnership for 21st Century Learning (founded by a coalition of business and educational leaders and policy makers) developed the *Framework for 21st Century Learning* to ensure K–12 students are prepared for the demands of the 21st century. The *Framework for 21st Century Learning*, created in collaboration with educators, nonprofits, foundations, and corporate members, describes outcomes and support systems designed to help K–12 students develop the skills and knowledge needed to succeed in the 21st-century global and technology-based workplace and society. The *Framework for 21st Century Learning* consists of two sections: Student Outcomes and Support Systems (Partnership for 21st Century Learning 2007). The 21st Century Student Outcomes are as follows:

1. Content Knowledge and 21st Century Themes
   Disciplines include English, reading or language arts; world languages; arts; mathematics; economics; science; geography; history; and government and civics. Twenty-first-century interdisciplinary themes include global awareness; financial, economic, business, and entrepreneurial literacy; civic literacy; health literacy; and environmental literacy.

2. Learning and Innovation Skills
   Emphasis is on creativity and innovation, critical thinking and problem solving, communication, and collaboration.

3. Information, Media, and Technology Skills
   This includes information literacy, media literacy, and information and communication technologies (ICT) literacy.

4. Life and Career Skills
   Students must be able to demonstrate flexibility and adaptability, initiative and self-direction, social and cross-cultural skills, productivity and accountability, and leadership and responsibility.

Table 1.1. How High-Impact Educational Practices Support the Essential Learning Outcomes

High-Impact Educational Practice	Fostering Broad Knowledge of Human Cultures and the Natural World	Strengthening Intellectual and Practical Skills	Deepening Personal and Social Responsibility	Practicing Integrative and Applied Learning
First-Year Seminars and Experiences (small group learning)		X		
Common Intellectual Experiences	X		X	
Learning Communities	X			X
Writing-Intensive Courses		X		
Collaborative Assignments and Projects		X	X	
Undergraduate Research	X	X		X
Diversity/Global Learning	X		X	
ePortfolios		X		X
Service-Learning, Community-Based Learning			X	X
Internships		X		X
Capstone Courses and Projects	X			X

The 21st Century Support Systems include:

1. 21st Century Standards

   Twenty-first-century standards focus on 21st-century skills (e.g., communication, collaboration, critical thinking, and creativity), content knowledge and expertise across academic subject areas, real-world learning and deep understanding, and active engagement in solving meaningful problems and allow for multiple measures of mastery.

2. Assessment of 21st Century Skills

   Multiple and balanced forms of assessment (including technology) should be used, including high-quality standardized testing and effective classroom formative and summative assessments; feedback should be embedded into everyday learning; and student portfolios should be used to demonstrate mastery of 21st-century skills to educators and prospective employers.

3. 21st Century Curriculum and Instruction

   Twenty-first-century skills are taught within key subjects, across content areas, and 21st-century interdisciplinary themes; emphasis is on competency-based learning, the integration of technology to support students' inquiry- and problem-based learning and higher order thinking skills, and learning beyond school walls.

4. 21st Century Professional Development

   Twenty-first-century professional development encourages and supports teachers to integrate 21st-century skills, tools, and teaching strategies into their classroom practice; focuses on balancing direct instruction with project-oriented teaching methods; emphasizes teaching for understanding to increase problem-solving, critical-thinking, and other 21st-century skills; provides professional learning communities for teachers; offers teachers support with identifying students' individual learning styles, intelligences, strengths and weaknesses, differentiated teaching and learning, and ongoing evaluation of students' 21st-century skills development.

5. 21st Century Learning Environments

   Twenty-first-century learning environments support the teaching and learning of 21st-century skills and collaboration among educators; provide equitable access to quality learning tools, technologies, and resources; and support team and individual learning, as well as community-based and international learning, in real-world, meaningful 21st-century contexts (e.g., project-based learning or other applied work) in face-to-face and online environments.

Additional information about the Partnership for 21st Century Learning and the *Framework for 21st Century Learning* can be found at http://www.p21.org/.

Although Kuh (2008) and others discuss the significance of high-impact educational practices at the college level, these practices are applicable to elementary and secondary levels of education as well. Just as the *Framework for 21st Century Learning* (Partnership for 21st Century Learning 2007) describes outcomes and support systems designed to ensure K–12 students are prepared to succeed in life and meet the demands of the 21st-century work environment, the LEAP initiative was launched by the AAC&U to align the goals for college learning with the needs of our new, global society (Kuh 2008). The purpose of the *Framework for 21st Century Learning* and the LEAP initiative is to help educators implement the practices and identify the outcomes that will best serve our students in a very diverse, global society. This includes recognizing our own students' diversity, culture, and individual needs.

The high-impact educational practices outlined by Kuh (2008) and the AAC&U can be paired to some of the outcomes and support systems discussed in the *Framework for 21st Century Learning* (see Table 1.2).

Although AAC&U's list of high-impact educational practices and the *Framework for 21st Century Learning* address different audiences and each has its own structure, common goals and outcomes stand out. For example, both emphasize the importance of global learning and global competence; collaborative learning; real-world learning; faculty-to-student and student-to-student relationships; fundamental subjects and courses; integrated studies that focus on broad and current themes; problem solving and critical thinking; literacy skills; and the application or demonstration of knowledge through writing, project-based learning, or other applied work.

Both AAC&U's list of high-impact educational practices and the *Framework for 21st Century Learning* emphasize the use of technology. AAC&U mentions the importance of ePortfolios (Watson, Kuh, Rhodes, Light, and Chen 2016), and the *Framework for 21st Century Learning* includes information, media, and technology skills as one of its student outcomes (Partnership for 21st Century Learning 2007). The Partnership for 21st Century Learning states that effective 21st-century citizens must be able to create, evaluate, and effectively utilize technology, specifying that students need to be information, media, and ICT literate. The Partnership for 21st Century Learning addresses technology use in the *Framework for 21st Century Learning*'s 21st Century Support Systems, also, noting technology's role in assessment, curriculum and instruction, and 21st-century learning environments. The International Society for Technology in Education (ISTE) Standards for Students specifically address how technology can be used to empower learners, produce digital citizens, create knowledge constructors, promote innovative designers, develop computational thinkers, support creative communicators, and support global collaborators (ISTE 2016). Although emphasis is not placed on high-impact educational practices, many of the indicators supporting the standards support high-impact educational practices, including indicators for global collaborators, creative communicators, knowledge constructors, and empowered learners. In addition, ISTE provides an ISTE Standards Community where educators can connect, share ideas, review practices, and discuss successes with each other. ISTE also offers a booklet that provides scenarios of what the standards look like in practice.

HIP TECHNOLOGY

HIP technology is the result of analyzing, evaluating, and integrating the relative aspects of the AAC&U High-Impact Educational Practices, the *Framework for 21st Century Learning*, and ISTE Standards for Students. Specifically, HIP technology examines how educators can use technology to support high-impact educational practices, including those that address just, equitable, and inclusive education; global learning; and designing and managing collaborative activities.

There are a variety of technologies available to support high-impact educational practices; however, as Kelly (2016) observes, the cycle of technology obsolescence is accelerating each day, so instead of relying on a particular app, device, or system to be around forever, educators need to consider the features that make technology worthwhile and instructionally sound. In time, better products will become available, improving upon what was and providing educators with options they may not have dreamed possible. As educators, we need to be critical consumers, innovators, reflective practitioners, and change agents in the use of technology and its impact on our students' lives. New and improved programs continue to make *newbies* out of all of us, no matter our age or experience (Kelly 2016).

Table 1.2. High-Impact Educational Practices Paired with Outcomes and Support Systems from the *Framework for 21st Century Learning*

Association of American Colleges & Universities High-Impact Educational Practices	The *Framework for 21st Century Learning* Student Outcomes and Support Systems
First-Year Seminars and Experiences *(e.g., students participate in small group experiences with faculty or staff)*	21st Century Learning Environments: Create learning practices, human support, and physical environments that will support the teaching and learning of 21st-century skill outcomes *(e.g., provide small group instruction; equitable access to quality learning tools, technologies, and resources; and a classroom that focuses on mutual respect)*
Common Intellectual Experiences *(e.g., students take a required set of common courses that include advanced integrative studies and/or participation in a learning community. Broad themes like technology and society and global interdependence are often combined)*	Content Knowledge and 21st Century Themes *(e.g., students master fundamental subjects, and 21st-century interdisciplinary themes are integrated into the curriculum—global awareness; financial, economic, business, and entrepreneurial literacy; civic literacy; health literacy; and environmental literacy)*
Learning Communities *(e.g., learning is integrated across courses and looks at matters beyond the classroom)*	Learning and Innovation Skills *(e.g., emphasis is on creativity and innovation, critical thinking and problem solving, communication, and collaboration)* 21st Century Learning Environments: Support expanded community and international involvement in learning, both face to face and online *(e.g., learning communities can include students from other regions, states, and countries)*
Writing-Intensive Courses *(e.g., writing at all levels of instruction and across the curriculum is emphasized)*	Information, Media, and Technology Skills *(e.g., students must be able to create, evaluate, and effectively utilize information, media, and technology)*
Collaborative Assignments and Projects *(e.g., study groups, team-based assignments, and cooperative projects and research are emphasized)*	Learning and Innovation Skills *(e.g., emphasis is on creativity and innovation, critical thinking and problem solving, communication, and collaboration)*
Undergraduate Research *(e.g., faculty engage students' learning through active involvement in systematic investigation and research that support key concepts and questions)*	21st Century Standards: Emphasize deep understanding rather than shallow knowledge; engage students with the real-world data, tools, and experts *(e.g., students learn best when actively engaged in solving meaningful problems)*
Diversity/Global Learning *(e.g., opportunities are provided to help students explore cultures, life experiences, and world views different from their own)*	Content Knowledge and 21st Century Themes *(e.g., students master fundamental subjects, and 21st-century interdisciplinary themes are integrated into the curriculum, including global awareness: students learn from and work collaboratively with others representing diverse cultures, religions, and lifestyles in a spirit of mutual respect and open dialogue in personal, work, and community context.*

(continued)

Table 1.2. (Continued)

Association of American Colleges & Universities High-Impact Educational Practices	The *Framework for 21st Century Learning* Student Outcomes and Support Systems
ePortfolios (e.g., *students assemble and reflect upon artifacts and instances of learning, with faculty guidance, to demonstrate required levels of competence*)	Learning and Innovation Skills (e.g., *emphasis is on creativity and innovation, critical thinking and problem solving, communication, and collaboration*) Information, Media, and Technology Skills (e.g., *students must be able to create, evaluate, and effectively use information, media, and technology*)
Service-Learning, Community-Based Learning (e.g., *field-based learning gives students the opportunity to apply what they are learning to real-world settings, as well as reflect on their experiences in a classroom setting*)	Life and Career Skills (e.g., *students develop thinking skills, content knowledge, and social and emotional competencies to navigate complex life and work environments*) 21st Century Learning Environments: Enable students to learn in relevant, real-world, 21st-century contexts (e.g., *students can engage in project-based or other applied work*)
Internships (e.g., *students are provided with direct experience in a work setting*)	Life and Career Skills (e.g., *students develop thinking skills, content knowledge, and social and emotional competencies to navigate complex life and work environments*) 21st Century Learning Environments: Enable students to learn in relevant, real-world, 21st-century contexts (e.g., *students can engage in project-based or other applied work*)
Capstone Courses and Projects (e.g., *students complete a culminating project that integrates and applies what they have learned*)	Assessment of 21st Century Skills: Enable development of portfolios of student work that demonstrate mastery of 21st-century skills to educators and prospective employers (e.g., *this can be technology based*)

At the beginning of this chapter, research was presented that suggests high-impact educational practices positively affect college students' learning, including their critical-thinking skills, intercultural effectiveness, and engagement. High-impact practices, such as small group instruction, collaborative, global, and service-learning, can positively affect K–12 students as well. For example, research shows small group instruction improves student engagement and the quality and accessibility of instruction in early childhood, elementary, and secondary education for children with and without disabilities, English and non-English learners, and children from all socioeconomic backgrounds (Coffey 2012; Hollo and Hirn 2015; Kruse, Spencer, Olszewski, and Goldstein 2015; Ledford and Wolery 2015; Quebec Fuentes 2013; Wasik 2008). Collaborative learning provides students the opportunity to co-construct knowledge, support each other's learning, and engage in the learning process. In addition, collaborative learning promotes critical-thinking and problem-solving skills, increased academic performance, students' social support, and learning about each other (Laal and Ghodsi 2012). Tomasello (2016) notes that "collaboration and collaborative learning are at the heart of both cultural learning and cultural creation" (650). Service-learning and global learning are other ways K–12 students can learn about themselves and the world around them. Service-learning projects support collaborative learning and student engagement, as well as help students think empathetically, reflectively, globally, and locally (Montgomery, Miller, Foss,

Tallakson, and Howard 2017; Ocal and Altınok 2016; Serriere, McGarry, Fuentes, and Mitra 2012; Walker 2015). Like service-learning, global learning is designed to meet standards and align with existing curriculum, as well as engage students in real-world problem solving. Global learning provides students with opportunities to critically think about, discuss, and reflect upon global issues such as sustainability, social justice and equity, intercultural understanding, human rights, and peace (Bourn 2016).

PREPARING OUR STUDENTS FOR THE FUTURE

High-impact educational practices benefit students at all levels. HIP technology is the process of using technology to support high-impact educational practices. Technology, like the demands on our society, changes over time. In addition, technology transforms society and adds to the transformative nature of our world, helping create a greater sense of global awareness and different cultures, heightened communication, and opportunities that never before existed. In his book, *The Inevitable*, Kelly (2016) discusses 12 technological forces that will greatly influence the future of society. Many of these forces are already taking place, but as technology continues to transform, advance, and proliferate throughout our society, so will these forces. Included in his discussion is the rapid advancement of artificial intelligence (AI), tracking, and virtual reality (VR). AI is already able to learn on its own and exists in products and services we use on a daily basis. The process of making objects increasingly smarter by integrating sensors and AI into them and connecting them to other AI systems is something Kelly refers to as *cognification*. Benefits of *cognifying* services or machines include outcomes like medical diagnoses without having to go to a doctor, self-driving cars, and robots that are able to perform tasks better than humans. The downside of cognification is the replacement of many jobs through automation, including what are considered white-collar jobs. Kelly identifies four categories of jobs that are likely to be replaced by robots: jobs humans can do, but robots can do even better (e.g., assemble cars); jobs humans can't do, but robots can (e.g., make 1,000 precise brass screws in an hour or less); jobs we didn't know we wanted to be done (e.g., drive a cart on Mars); and jobs only humans can do—at first (e.g., as technology evolves, as it did during the Industrial Revolution, humans will be free of certain tasks and will ask themselves again, "What are humans for?" creating new purposes and opportunities to pursue). In many cases, we are preparing our students for jobs that do not yet exist, making high-impact educational practices much more important.

As technology continues to evolve, we can use advances in AI, tracking, VR, and other inevitable forces to help meet the needs of our students and prepare them for the future. AI systems can support students' learning, advanced tracking can help monitor students' success, and VR can provide students with opportunities to collaborate and experience real-world situations and environments that may not otherwise be available or exist. Given technology continues to evolve and change at a rapid pace, our focus should not be on a specific program, device, or app but rather on how we can provide meaningful, transformative, and inclusive learning experiences for our students.

TECHNOLOGY STANDARDS AND FRAMEWORKS

Technology continues to be an inevitable force that shapes the future; therefore, in addition to the *Framework for 21st Century Learning*, it is important to be mindful of the ISTE Standards, as well as the *K–12 Computer Science Framework*. ISTE has been a leader in advancing K–12 educational technology use for many years. Started over 40 years ago by a small group of K–12 teachers and University of Oregon faculty, ISTE is now a worldwide network of educators who work together to support professional growth in and effective use of technology in K–12 education. Over the years, they have created professional learning networks, developed technology-based journals, held annual conferences, and developed technology standards that are used throughout K–12 schools and at the university level. As of 2018, ISTE has five sets of standards. These include the ISTE Standards for Students, Educators, Administrators, Coaches, and Computer Science Educators. The ISTE Standards for Students, as mentioned previously, address how technology can be used to empower learners, produce digital citizens, create knowledge constructors, promote innovative designers, develop computational thinkers, support creative communicators, and support global collaborators. The ISTE Standards for Educators focus on the educator as a learner, leader, citizen, collaborator, designer, facilitator, and analyst. The ISTE Standards for Administrators discuss traits of administrators as technology leaders for their schools. For example, they should be visionary leaders in the integration of technology, promote a digital-age learning culture, provide an environment of professional practices where educators have the time and resources to participate in professional development and improve their technology practices, ensure systematic improvements, and model and facilitate digital citizenship. The ISTE Standards for Coaches address the role of teacher technology leaders. They, too, must provide visionary leadership, as well as assist teachers with teaching, learning, and assessments of technology; support digital-age learning environments; provide professional development and program evaluation; model and promote digital citizenship; and continually expand their content knowledge and professional growth in technology. The ISTE Standards for Computer Science Educators focus on knowledge of content, effective teaching and learning strategies (e.g., collaborative learning and real-world problems), effective learning environments, and effective professional knowledge and skills. Additional information about the ISTE Standards can be found at https://www.iste.org/.

The *K–12 Computer Science Framework* is a document designed to guide states in the development of computer science standards. The *K–12 Computer Science Framework* was created by the Computer Science Teachers Association, Cyber Innovation Center, the Association for Computing Machinery, Code.org, and National Math and Science Initiative in collaboration with states, districts, and the computer science education community. The *K–12 Computer Science Framework* describes what students should know and what students should do in order for states and others to create performance expectations or standards for computer science. The authors of the *K–12 Computer Science Framework* discuss how computer science is often confused with computing education, which includes computer literacy, educational technology, information technology, digital citizenship, and computer science (K–12 Computer Science Framework 2016). Computer literacy refers to the general use of programs and computers, such as knowing how to use a multimedia program or the Internet. Educational technology is the use of computer literacy in school subjects, for example, using the Internet to research information and using a multimedia program to demonstrate what one learned about an assigned topic (e.g., depletion of the rain forest). Informational technology (IT) typically addresses the industrial applications of computer science but focuses more on collecting data, creating networks, maintaining systems, and installing software rather than creating it. IT professionals often have experience in computer science. Digital citizenship refers to the responsible, ethical, and appropriate use of technology. Computer science is knowing how and why computers work.

The *K–12 Computer Science Framework* provides five core concepts and seven core practices that should be used in the development of computer science standards (see Table 1.3).

Noting the inequities that currently exist in the field of computer science and who participates in and has access to computer science courses, the authors of the *K–12 Computer Science Framework* write:

> First and foremost, the K–12 Computer Science Framework is designed for all students, regardless of their age, race, gender, disability, or socioeconomic status. The structure

Table 1.3. Core Concepts and Practices for the Development of Computer Science Standards

Core Concepts	Core Practices
Computing Systems	Fostering an Inclusive Computing Culture
Networks and the Internet	Collaborating Around Computing
Data Analysis	Recognizing and Defining Computational Problems
Algorithms and Programming	Developing and Using Abstractions
Impacts of Computing	Creating Computational Artifacts
	Testing and Refining Computational Artifacts
	Communicating About Computing

Source: *K–12 Computer Science Framework*. 2016. Retrieved from http://www.k12cs.org. Reprinted with permission.

> and content of the framework reflect the need for diversity in computing and attention to issues of equity, including accessibility. The choice of Impacts of Computing as one of the core concepts and Fostering an Inclusive Computing Culture as one of the core practices make diversity, equity, and accessibility key topics of study, in addition to interweaving them through the other concepts and practices. (K–12 Computer Science Framework 2016, 15)

In addition to establishing a framework that addresses accessibility, inequity, and stereotypes, the authors discuss research regarding the importance of early engagement in computer science, providing practical applications of the *K–12 Computer Science Framework*'s concepts and practices for the pre-K setting.

SUMMARY

High-impact educational practices include practices that emphasize collaborative learning, critical inquiry, information literacy, frequent writing, and other skills that develop students' intellectual competencies and real-world learning. High-impact educational practices benefit students at all levels. HIP technology examines how educators can use technology to support high-impact educational practices. Because technology continues to evolve and change at a rapid pace, HIP technology does not focus on using specific computer programs, devices, or apps but rather on how technology can be used to support high-impact educational practices, helping prepare students for the needs of the 21st-century global community and workforce.

Technology standards and frameworks have been written to help educators prepare students to be successful in the 21st century. ISTE Standards are available for Students, Educators, Administrators, Coaches, and Computer Science Educators. The *Framework for 21st Century Learning* describes outcomes and support systems designed to ensure K–12 students are prepared to meet the demands of the 21st century, and the *K–12 Computer Science Framework* is designed to guide states in the development of computer science standards. Both frameworks discuss the importance of inclusive and accessible education.

ACTIVITIES

1. Think back to your experience as an undergraduate student. What, if any, high-impact educational practices do you recall? How did these practices, or lack of practices, affect your education or experience as an undergraduate student? Share and compare your experiences with a fellow student or colleague.

2. Think back to your experience as a K–12 student. What, if any, high-impact educational practices do you recall? How did these practices, or lack of practices, affect your education or experience as a K–12 student? Share and compare your experiences with a fellow student or colleague, and how this affects or will affect your teaching.

3. Work with a partner or small group to explore the Partnership for 21st Century Learning website at http://www.p21.org/. In addition to taking a closer look at the *Framework for 21st Century Learning*, decide on and assign different parts of the website for your partner(s) to explore. Come back together as a group, and share what you learned. Present what you found most interesting or helpful to the class.

4. In the following clip, Kevin Kelly discusses three of his "12 Inevitable Tech Forces That Will Shape Our Future": https://youtu.be/pZwq8eMdYrY.
   After watching the video, reflect on the questions in the Ch1. Resource Page: Kevin Kelly at the end of this chapter. Summarize your thoughts, and share and compare your analysis with others.

5. Work with a small group (no more than four members) to become an expert on one of the ISTE Standards for Students. Each group should choose a different standard and present their findings and recommendations to the class. See the Ch1. Resource Page: ISTE Standards at the end of this chapter for more information.

6. Check to see if your school, district, and/or state use the ISTE technology standards. How are they aligned with student instruction, professional development, and the school's technology plan? Present your findings to your classmates, as well as your praises, recommendations, and concerns regarding the use of technology at your school. Include how technology is or isn't being used to support high-impact educational practices.

7. Go to https://k12cs.org/ and take time to learn more about the *K–12 Computer Science Framework*. While you are on the website, view the video (also at https://youtu.be/CD0EIGfr950) available on the home page. In addition, download the *K–12 Computer Science Framework*, and read the Executive Summary and Chapters 1, 2, 8, and 9. Feel free to read or skim the other chapters. Lastly, go back to the website and click on "See the concepts and practices." Choose a grade band, and review the outcomes. Based upon what you watched and read, what stands out most to you and why? Identify what you feel are the most critical elements or important messages of each of the chapters. In addition, share your thoughts/reflect upon how curriculum may change as a result of implementing computer science standards. Share and compare your response with your classmates.

8. Check to see if your school, district, and/or state has computer science standards. How are they aligned with the *K–12 Computer Science Framework*? What improvements or changes would you make on the basis of what you learned about the *K–12 Computer Science Framework*? Share your findings and reflection with your peers.

RESOURCE LIST

Association of American Colleges & Universities (AAC&U): https://www.aacu.org/resources/high-impact-practices

Framework for 21st Century Learning: http://www.p21.org/

International Society for Technology in Education (ISTE): https://www.iste.org/

K–12 Computer Science Framework: https://k12cs.org/

REFERENCES

Bonet, G. and Walters, B. R. 2016. High impact practices: Student engagement and retention. *College Student Journal, 50*(2), 224–235.

Bourn, D. 2016. Global learning and the school curriculum. *Management in Education, 30*(3), 121–125.

BrckaLorenz, A., Garvey, J. C., Hurtado, S. S., and Latopolski, K. 2017. High-impact practices and student–faculty interactions for gender-variant students. *Journal of Diversity in Higher Education, 10*(4), 350–365.

Coffey, G. 2012. Literacy and technology: Integrating technology with small group, peer-led discussions of literature. *International Electronic Journal of Elementary Education, 4*(2), 395–405.

Hollo, A. and Hirn, R. G. 2015. Teacher and student behaviors in the contexts of grade level and instructional grouping. *Preventing School Failure, 59*(1), 30–39.

International Society for Technology in Education. 2016. ISTE Standards for Students [online]. Available at: https://www.iste.org/standards/standards-for-students. Accessed on September 18, 2017.

Kelly, K. 2016. *The inevitable*. New York, NY: Viking Press.

Kilgo, C. A., Ezell Sheets, J. K., and Pascarella, E. T. 2015. The link between high-impact practices and student learning: Some longitudinal evidence. *Higher Education: The International Journal of Higher Education and Educational Planning, 69*(4), 509–525.

Kruse, L. G., Spencer, T. D., Olszewski, A., and Goldstein, H. 2015. Small groups, big gains: Efficacy of a tier 2 phonological awareness intervention with preschoolers with early literacy deficits. *American Journal of Speech-Language Pathology (Online), 24*(2), 189–205.

K–12 Computer Science Framework. 2016. *K–12 Computer Science Framework* [online]. Available at: https://k12cs.org/. Accessed on September 19, 2017.

Kuh, G. D. 2008. *High-impact educational practices: What they are, who has access to them, and why they matter*. Washington, DC: Association of American Colleges & Universities.

Laal, M. and Ghodsi, S. M. 2012. Benefits of collaborative learning. *Procedia—Social and Behavioral Sciences, 31*, 486–490.

Ledford, J. R. and Wolery, M. 2015. Observational learning of academic and social behaviors during small-group direct instruction. *Exceptional Children, 81*(3), 272–291.

Miller, A. L., Rocconi, L. M., and Dumford, A. D. 2017. Focus on the finish line: Does high-impact practice participation influence career plans and early job attainment?*Higher Education, 75*(3), 489–506.

Montgomery, S. E., Miller, W., Foss, P., Tallakson, D., and Howard, M. 2017. Banners for books: "Mighty-hearted" kindergartners take action through arts-based service learning. *Early Childhood Education Journal, 45*(1), 1–14.

Ocal, A. and Altınok, A. 2016. Developing social sensitivity with service-learning. *Social Indicators Research, 129*(1), 61–75.

Partnership for 21st Century Learning. 2007. *Framework for 21st Century Learning* [online]. Available at: http://www.p21.org/our-work/p21-framework. Accessed on September 18, 2017.

Quebec Fuentes, S. 2013. Small-group discourse: Establishing a communication-rich classroom. *Clearing House: A Journal of Educational Strategies, Issues and Ideas, 86*(3), 93–98.

Serriere, S., McGarry, L., Fuentes, D., and Mitra, D. 2012. How service-learning can ignite thinking. *Social Studies and the Young Learner, 24*(4), 6–10.

Tomasello, M. 2016. Cultural learning redux. *Child Development, 87*(3), 643–653.

Walker, A. B. 2015. Giving literacy, learning literacy: Service-learning and school book drives. *Reading Teacher, 69*(3), 299–306.

Wasik, B. 2008. When fewer is more: Small groups in early childhood classrooms. *Early Childhood Education Journal, 35*(6), 515–521.

Watson, C. E., Kuh, G. D., Rhodes, T., Light, T. P., and Chen, H. L. 2016. Editorial: ePortfolios—The eleventh high impact practice. *International Journal of ePortfolio, 6*(2), 65–69.

Ch1. Resource Page: Kevin Kelly

View https://youtu.be/pZwq8eMdYrY
12 Inevitable Tech Forces That Will Shape Our Future by Kevin Kelly
After watching the video, reflect on the following questions. Summarize your thoughts and share and compare your analysis with others.

- What did you find most intriguing about AI?

- What are your concerns, if any, about AI?

- How do you see AI affecting learning and instruction in the future? Provide examples.

- How do you see AI affecting your students' future—including needs, job skills, and occupations—in regard to efficiency and inefficiency?

- What did you find most intriguing about VR?

- What are your concerns, if any, about VR?

- How do you see VR affecting learning and instruction in the future? Provide examples.

- What do you believe are the pros and cons of how VR may affect social experiences?

- What did you find most intriguing about tracking?

- What are your concerns, if any, about tracking?

- How do you see advanced tracking affecting learning and instruction in the future? Provide examples.

The ISTE Standards for Students are available at:
http://www.iste.org/standards/for-students
Work with a small group (no more than four members) to become an "expert" on one of the ISTE Standards for Students. Each group should choose a different standard and present their findings and recommendations to the class.

Here is your group task:
Using your favorite presentation tool, be prepared to discuss your standard with your peers. Your presentation should consist of the following:

- Introduction, including group members' names and contributions to the project.

- An overview of your standard and indicators.

- At least seven resources for helping educators teach the standard. Resources could be websites, articles, software, apps, and so forth. Discuss and share these resources. You'll note that ISTE offers definitions throughout its standards through underlined words. These terms can help as you are researching for different software or resource options.

- A sample lesson plan that focuses on at least one of the indicators. Make sure you identify the indicator(s) and include the necessary modifications and accommodations to ensure all of your students can succeed. You may choose any content area. For example, you may choose to do a social studies lesson that involves students learning about their peers in another country via ePals (if your standard is Global Collaborator). Or, you may have your students create an iMovie to demonstrate how they solved a complex math problem (if your standard is Creative Communicator). If you are not able to teach the lesson, you should still provide your peers with a detailed overview of how the lesson begins, management plans, what the students will be doing and learning, how you will address the needs of different learners, and how you will assess students' work. If you and your teammates have access to a classroom and can teach the lesson, include your reflection of how the lesson went, as well as sample student work.

- When you create your lesson plan, include a *final thoughts* section to share how your use of technology is helping your students understand, communicate, or collaborate better—not just differently. What is the impact or purpose of the technology? Also, address how you will ensure you know the technology well enough and have the resources necessary to use it effectively with your students.

- Conclude with your final thoughts and recommendations regarding teaching your selected standard.

- It is important to remember that technology serves a purpose; the purpose is not to serve technology. As an educator, ask yourself, "How can this technology (e.g., software application, app, website, and device) support my students' learning? Is it just something fun or novel that focuses more on the amusing or different aspects of the technology or does it serve a learning purpose? Will it help my students understand, communicate, or collaborate better?" If the answer is yes, the next question is, "How can I ensure I know the technology well enough and have the resources necessary to use it effectively with my students?"

- Your presentation should be 15–20 minutes. One member of your team will submit your presentation and lesson plan on the day you present.

Chapter 2

Collaborative Assignments and Projects

OVERVIEW

Working together provides students with the opportunity to benefit from the knowledge and experiences of others, share responsibility, view problems and situations from different perspectives, learn cooperation and how to compromise, and to be accountable to others. These are important 21st-century skills; "collaboration is taking over the workplace" (Cross, Rebele, and Grant 2016, 1). By providing students with opportunities to collaborate in pairs, small groups, and cooperative learning activities, educators can help students learn more than just content. Students learn the importance of listening, respecting and working with others who may be different from themselves, and other social skills.

This chapter focuses on the high-impact educational practices of small group instruction and collaborative and cooperative learning. The chapter begins by discussing how to design and manage small group instruction, how the Center for Research on Education, Diversity, and Excellence (CREDE) Professional Development Model may help teachers progress to small group instruction, and how technology can support small group instruction. Next, designing and managing collaborative activities, including cooperative learning, is discussed. Benefits and challenges of face-to-face and online collaborative and cooperative learning are examined, and guidelines for facilitating small group discourse and managing online discussions are provided. Four types of cooperative learning (formal cooperative learning, informal cooperative learning, cooperative base groups, and constructive controversy) are introduced and defined with examples. Lastly, benefits and pitfalls of cooperative group learning are addressed, followed by examples of how technology can support collaborative and cooperative group learning.

DESIGNING AND MANAGING SMALL GROUP INSTRUCTION

Small group instruction provides teachers with the opportunity to provide additional support to their students, focusing on their individual needs. There are many benefits of small group instruction. These include increased student-to-student and teacher-to-student interactions, improved academic achievement, better quality and accessibility of instruction, and shared cultural learning (Coffey 2012; Hollo and Hirn 2015; Kruse, Spencer, Olszewski, and Goldstein 2015; Ledford and Wolery 2015; Quebec Fuentes 2013; Tomasello 2016; Wasik 2008). Although there are many benefits of small group instruction, guidelines are usually necessary to help students stay on task and actively participate in the group. For example, teachers will want to establish and explicitly teach rules and routines for participating in the small group and review these rules regularly. Rules may include how to take turns, show respect, what to bring to the group, and so on. For small group discussions, Beaulieu-Jones and Proctor (2016) recommend letting students speak freely when they

Table 2.1. Guidelines for Creating Small, Instructional Groups

Guideline	Rationale
No group should exceed five students.	Larger groups make it difficult to provide individualized instruction.
The learning goal of the activity should dictate the number of students in a small group.	Depending on the activity and ability of the students, some groups may be smaller.
Groups should be intentionally organized.	Deliberately grouping students allows teachers to work with students who need to complete a specific goal or work on a specific skill.
Small group instruction should be distinct from center time activities.	In small group instruction, the teacher plays an active role with the students, engaging them in activities and teaching specific concepts and ideas. In center activities, students explore concepts with other students, manipulating objects, conducting experiments on their own, and participating in other inquiry-based, hands-on activities.
Teach content in small groups rather than in whole groups.	One-to-one instruction supports the teaching and learning of early literacy, math, and science concepts.
Ensure teachers have an active role in the small group experience.	One of the most valuable aspects of small group instruction is the increased opportunity for students and teachers to interact with each other.
Make sure small group instruction is built into the daily schedule.	Building small group instruction into the daily schedule allows all students to participate in small group instruction at least once a week.

have something to say, as long as they do not speak over another person. They also encourage teachers to let students know it is okay to disagree with each other, but students should disagree in a respectful manner using language such as "I respectfully disagree because . . . ," "I see why you think that, but . . .," "That is a good point, but I have a different idea. . . ." Modeling appropriate language is very important. Teachers may take the opportunity during small group instruction to reinforce language skills also, as well as provide students with shared language and other cultural experiences.

Wasik (2008) provides seven guidelines for creating small, instructional groups for young learners, although small group instruction can be beneficial at any level (see Table 2.1).

In addition, Wasik (2008) reminds teachers that the impact of small group instruction depends on how well teachers plan for small group instruction. Teachers need to identify the group size and members, the concepts to be taught, and the materials that will be used to teach the concepts and plan the discussion questions.

In face-to-face environments, working with a small group of students can be challenging if the other students in the classroom are not engaged. Teachers need to establish routines, set expectations, and manage a classroom environment that supports student independence. This can be done by dividing the whole class into small groups that rotate through different centers or work together on another assignment (e.g., a multimedia project), by structuring individual or paired assignments and activities, or providing a whole class activity. Examples of individual assignments include having students work independently on Accelerated Reader, ST (JiJi) Math, or other computer-mediated activity designed to meet students' individual needs. Students can work in pairs or individually on Code.org (https://code.org) or Made with Code (https://www.madewithcode.com/) to learn and enhance their computer programming skills, on reading or writing assignments, or on other activities that engage them and require little or no intervention. It may help to assign classroom leaders who can assist students who have a specific question that may not require the teacher's guidance. Assigning classroom leaders or using the approach "ask three before you ask me" may also help when assigning a whole class activity during small group instruction. When students are assigned to work on their own (i.e., whether independently, in pairs or small groups, or as a whole class), clear expectations for behavior and outcomes are critical, as is the students' ability to complete their assigned tasks. Modeling, rehearsing, repeating, and reviewing are approaches teachers can use to help establish routines and expectations for their students.

CREDE Professional Development Model

One model that may help teachers progress to small group instruction is the CREDE Professional Development Model. The CREDE Professional Development Model is designed to help teachers transform their teaching practices from traditional whole group teaching to small interactive groups (Wyatt and Chapman-DeSousa 2017). It consists of five phases. See Table 2.2 (Wyatt and Chapman-DeSousa 2017, 63).

Teachers work through each phase, progressing to the next phase when they feel ready to proceed. Teachers work with professional development coaches to assist them through each phase. Wyatt and Chapman-DeSousa (2017) state the model is based on extensive research that examines

Table 2.2. Phases of CREDE Model

CREDE Phase	Description of Phase
Phase 1	The teacher designs activities that engage learners in peer-to-peer collaboration with the goal of redefining teaching and learning as joint productive activity.
Phase 2	The learners are divided in half, so that one half works with the teacher, while the other half engages in an independent activity. After a set amount of time, the two groups rotate.
Phase 3	The classroom is organized into multiple simultaneous activities in which learners work independently, while the teacher floats to address any concerns. After spending a specified amount of time in an activity, the learners rotate to a new center, until the students have completed all activities.
Phase 4	A teacher center emerges in which a small group engages with the teacher, while the rest of the learners are organized into independent activity centers. The teacher models academic language and new ways of thinking and encourages learners to work together, while learners at the other centers rely on each other for assistance to accomplish tasks. After a set amount of time, the learners rotate to new centers.
Phase 5	The teacher center is transformed into an Instructional Conversation (IC), which are less teacher directed and more discussion based. ICs focus on developing students' cognitive and linguistic skills.

best teaching practices for culturally and linguistically diverse learners and is especially effective for classrooms with high levels of diversity.

How Technology Can Support Small Group Instruction

As mentioned earlier, for students waiting for small group instruction, technology can provide individualized instruction through programs like ST (JiJi) Math, Accelerated Reader, and other instructional programs; paired learning can take place on sites like Code.org (https://code.org), Made with Code (https://www.madewithcode.com/), or Alice (http://www.alice.org/) to enhance students' computer science skills; student pairs can conduct research on the Internet for an assigned project; and student teams can work on assigned multimedia projects. Technology can also help teachers facilitate small group instruction. Teachers may use mobile devices as part of small group instruction, taking advantage of interactive whiteboard apps and other instructional tools to engage students. Interactive whiteboard examples include ShowMe, BaiBoard, and Educreations Interactive Whiteboard. Many more can be found by searching for "interactive whiteboard apps." In addition to recording instruction, several interactive whiteboard apps have built-in multimedia features, including voice-over, and collaboration features. Evernote, Google Keep, and other programs can be used for record keeping during small group instruction. Teachers can facilitate small group instruction online using Zoom, Skype, or other videoconferencing software, as well as online forums, chat rooms, and programs like VoiceThread. In some cases, small group, computer-assisted instruction can be more effective than or just as effective as one-to-one tutoring by teachers (Chambers, Slavin, Madden, Abrami, Logan, and Gifford 2011). BrckaLorenz, Garvey, Hurtado, and Latopolski (2017) note, however, the importance of positive teacher-student interactions for increased participation in high-impact educational practices, especially for gender variant students.

DESIGNING AND MANAGING COLLABORATIVE ACTIVITIES, INCLUDING COOPERATIVE LEARNING

Collaborative learning occurs when groups of students help each other learn. This can take place online or face to face. There are several benefits of peer-led, online discussion groups (Coffey 2012; Comer and Lenaghan 2013):

- Student motivation and engagement are increased.

- Learners can connect outside of the classroom.

- Learning is improved.

- Online group activities can foster social interactions and a community of learners.

- Transcripts are available for review and analysis by the students and teacher.

Asynchronous discussions provide additional benefits, including:

- Group members have an opportunity to be heard without being interrupted.

- Students have more time to formulate their thoughts and respond, giving marginalized students (e.g., linguistically diverse, shy) a voice in the discussion.

- Students who tend not to participate in the traditional classroom are required to contribute.

- Students have more opportunities for interaction and to consider different points of view.

- Discussions can be more in depth.

Challenges of online discussions include access, tone (if text only), and issues of speed (if groups are synchronous). Although access to computers and the Internet has increased dramatically, access still needs to be considered when assigning online projects. Teachers need to ensure their students have reliable Internet access and a device that can access it outside of the classroom. According to the Organisation for Economic Co-Operation and Development (OECD 2015), over 94 percent of homes in the United States have a least one computer and 99.7 percent have Internet access. Only 79.8 percent of disadvantaged students have Internet access. This can be problematic if teachers are expecting students to complete Internet activities outside of school. The tone of online messages can be problematic too. This problem can be mediated with strategic use of pictographs such as emojis and emoticons. Küster (2016) states that emoji are icons that "represent emotions, feelings, or activities," and emoticons "(from 'emotion' plus 'icon') are specifically intended to depict facial expression or body posture as a way of conveying emotion or attitude in e-mail and text messages" (14). Lastly, issues of speed can be a challenge when trying to type and keep current with online chats. Students may lack the typing and reading skills necessary to keep up with the multiple discussion threads (Day and Kroon 2010).

Designing effective online collaborative discussion groups requires teachers to encourage posts and responses that are thoughtful, consider classmates' viewpoints, are constructive, and address the provided prompt(s). Cursory or repetitious comments should be avoided. Based on the work of Comer and Lenaghan (2013), recommendations for designing and managing online discussions include:

- Discuss, model, and provide examples of effective posts and responses. Teachers may have students practice posts and responses before grading them.

- Provide prompts that apply course concepts to students' own experiences in ways that support meaningful discussion about course material. Student responses should incorporate original examples (OEs) tied to their own experiences.

- Encourage students to analyze and reflect on their classmates' posts to provide value-added comments (VACs)—useful advice, solutions, and constructive feedback.

- Ensure students who are not the first to post a VAC read previous VACs so repetition does not occur. Previous VACs should also be considered and incorporated into new VACs.

- Plan time for students to synthesize and reflect on VACs they received and elaborate or continue discussions with the classmates.

In addition to setting up the prompts, providing guidelines, and clarifying expectations, the instructor's role is to monitor the discussion—as the instructor would in a face-to-face collaborative group discussion, intervening to correct inaccuracies, to provide value-added information or stimulate students' thinking and reasoning, or to ensure civility. When addressing cases of incivility, it is important to handle the situation privately and to remind students of proper netiquette, respect, and the importance of acknowledging multiple perspectives. The instructor's presence is important but not to the point of dominating the discussion (Comer and Lenaghan 2013). Weekly summations of the groups' discussions can be insightful to the students and provide instructor presence too.

Table 2.3. Guidelines for Facilitating Face-to-Face Small Group Discourse

Event	Suggestion
If students in a group cannot work without the presence of the teacher or dominant student	• Ask students to specifically state their questions • Redirect those questions to the group • Encourage students to direct their explanations to their group members rather than you • Refer students to other resources such as notes, definitions, or hints
If you help a group communicate about a problem, but they cease talking when you depart	• Leave the group with a task that requires them to communicate, such as comparing solution strategies • Return to the group to follow up on their progress with the task
If students in a group are all working independently	• Allow them to work independently initially • Then ask them to explain and compare strategies
If you notice a mistake(s) in students' work, use the error as an opportunity for inquiry by	• Modeling the process of evaluating work without directly identifying the error • Asking students to compare and evaluate each other's work
If you need an appropriate first question when a group asks for help and you are unaware of their progress on a task	• Ask the group to explain what has been done so far
If a student unsuccessfully tries to help another student	• Ask the student being helped to restate the explanation in his or her own words • Follow up by asking the student who helped whether he or she agrees with the restatement of his or her reasoning
If there is a student in a group that dominates the group discussion	• Ask the other students to restate in their own words the ideas of the dominant student • Highlight other students' ideas that are overlooked by the dominant student
If students rush to complete a task	• Ask students to compare their strategies • Ask students to evaluate each other's work
If students in a group view the teacher as the only resource to answer their questions	• Ask students to redirect their questions to their group members • Encourage students to explain their work to others • Ask students to evaluate each other's work
If students blindly accept the incorrect work of another student	• Ask students to restate the explanation in their own words • Ask students to evaluate the other students' incorrect idea

In small group instruction, teachers play a direct role in the small group. The teacher's role during collaborative and cooperative learning activities is usually as a guide or a coach, whether it is online or face to face. Teachers may interact with student groups by probing students' thinking and reasoning, encouraging students to elaborate and ask each other additional questions, and monitoring groups' progress. Guidelines for facilitating face-to-face, small group discourse are presented in Table 2.3 (Quebec Fuentes 2013, 97).

Collaborative and cooperative learning provide many benefits, including social, psychological, and academic benefits. For example, collaborative and cooperative group learning helps to reduce stereotypes, can reduce anxiety and make learning more interesting, and promotes higher achievement (Bertucci, Conte, Johnson, and Johnson 2010; Laal and Ghodsi 2012). Although the terms *collaborative* and *cooperative* group learning are often used interchangeably and both *collaborative* and *cooperative* group learning have many of the same benefits, researchers suggest they are distinct. Cooperative learning typically occurs in primary schools, but cooperative learning can be effective at any grade level (Hossain, Tarmizi, and Ayud 2012; Nam and Zellner 2011; Slavin 2013; Wallhead and Dyson 2017). Bruffee (1995) and Rockwood (1995a, 1995b) note that cooperative learning provides more structure to help children from different backgrounds, ability groups, and so on to learn to work together toward a common goal. Teachers usually structure the learning groups (e.g., determine the size and which students will be in each group), assign students roles or tasks within each group, and teach collaboration and social skills. Johnson and Johnson (1999, 2009) suggest that a cooperative learning group has five defining characteristics:

1. Positive Interdependence: There is a group goal to maximize all members' learning beyond their individual abilities; members succeed only if the other members in their group succeed.

2. Individual Accountability: Group members hold themselves and each other accountable for high-quality work; students are held accountable for their share of the work.

3. Promotive Interaction: Group members produce joint products, providing both academic and personal support; students promote each other's learning.

4. Social Skills: Group members are taught social skills and are expected to use them to coordinate their efforts; teamwork and task work are emphasized.

5. Group Processing: Groups analyze how well they are achieving their goals, working together, and learning.

Collaborative learning, on the other hand, is designed for older students and adults (Bruffee 1995; Rockwood 1995a, 1995b) or in situations where teacher guidance is minimal or not necessary once the goals and expectations of assignment have been communicated (McInnerney and Roberts 2005). Teachers do not monitor students' behavior, teach social skills, or oversee contributions to the group. Group members govern themselves and pursue the task as they see fit. The teacher is available to answer questions, but it is up to the students to determine how they will approach the given assignment, what tasks need to be accomplished, who is doing what task, and how they will manage their time to ensure the assignment is completed on time. Bruffee (1995, 17) notes:

Collaborative learning replaces the traditional classroom social structure with another structure: negotiated relationships among students and a negotiated relationship between those student communities and the teacher. By cultivating students' interdependence, this alternative classroom social structure helps students become autonomous, articulate, and socially and intellectually mature, and it helps them learn the substance at issue not as conclusive *facts* but as the constructed result of a disciplined social process of inquiry.

Collaborative learning supports self-regulated learning and engagement, affecting students' cognitive, motivational, and socioemotional aspects of learning (Järvelä, Järvenoja, Malmberg, Isohätälä, and Sobocinski 2016).

Both cooperative and collaborative learning groups require interdependence and are student centered, but collaborative learning places more emphasis on students' social growth and group independence. Groups may experience what Behfar, Mannix, Peterson, and Trochim (2011) describe as *process conflict*. Process conflict occurs when group members disagree on how to distribute work, set timelines or work schedules, and confront group members who do not contribute or submit work as agreed. Similar *pitfalls* can occur in cooperative learning groups. Some researchers suggest the terms *cooperative* and *collaborative* groups should be synonymous, noting that there is tremendous overlap between the two types of groups (Jacobs 2015). Each approach provides students with more control over their own learning, supports students working with and learning about others, requires some teacher intervention or monitoring (e.g., setting milestones for certain aspects of the assignment), requires students to engage in higher-order thinking skills and develop their interpersonal communication skills, and helps to develop a community of learners.

Cooperative Learning Techniques

Johnson and Johnson (2014) describe four types of cooperative learning: formal cooperative learning, informal cooperative learning, cooperative base groups, and constructive controversy (see Table 2.4).

As noted in Table 2.4, there are a variety of formal cooperative group techniques, including Student Teams Achievement Divisions, Teams Games Tournament, Team-Assisted Individualization, Jigsaw, Group Investigation, and Learning Together (Slavin 1994, 1999, 2011; Vermette 1998):

Student Teams Achievement Divisions (STAD)—Students learn something as a team, contribute to the team by improving their own past performance, and earn team rewards based on their improvements. Students are usually heterogeneously mixed by ability and take individual weekly quizzes. For example, student teams may study about the Westward Movement and take weekly quizzes on the content. Teams earn points based on each student's improvement from previous quizzes. If a student scores 5 out of 10 points on the first quiz and 8 out of 10 on the second quiz, he or she may earn 8 points for his or her team, plus 2 bonus points for improving. If a student scores 7 out of 10 points on the first quiz and 5 out of 10 on the second quiz, he or she may earn 5 points for his or her team but no bonus points. If a student scores 10 points on both quizzes, he or she may earn a total of 12 points (10 points for the second quiz plus 2 bonus points for the perfect score) for his or her team.

Teams Games Tournament (TGT)—Similar to STAD except that weekly tournaments replace weekly quizzes. Homogeneous, three-member teams are formed from the existing heterogeneous groups and compete against similar ability groups to earn points for their regular, heterogeneous group. As with STAD, high-performing teams earn group rewards. For example, existing heterogeneous groups may contain one each low-, average-, and high-ability student. During weekly tournaments (e.g., a game of Jeopardy), low-ability students form groups of three, average-ability students form groups of three, and high-ability students form groups of three. Low-ability groups compete against each other, average-ability groups compete against each other, and high-ability groups compete against each other. The winning homogeneous groups earn points for their heterogeneous teams.

Team-Assisted Individualization (TAI)—Combines cooperative learning with individualized instruction. Students are placed into groups but work at their own pace and level. Team members check each other's work and help one another with problems. Teams earn points based on the individual performance of each member in the group. Team members encourage and support one another because they want their teams to succeed (Slavin 1994). For example, students at different spelling levels may be placed into heterogeneous groups. The group may consist of one low speller,

Table 2.4. Different Types of Cooperative Learning

Type of Cooperative Learning	Description	Examples
Formal Cooperative Learning	Students work together in arranged small groups for one class period to several weeks, working toward common learning goals and mutually completing specific tasks and assignments.	Student Teams Achievement Divisions, Teams Games Tournament, Team-Assisted Individualization, Jigsaw, Group Investigation, and Learning Together
Informal Cooperative Learning	Students work together to achieve a common learning goal in temporary, ad hoc groups that last from a few minutes to one class period.	Think-Pair-Share, Peer Instruction, Whole Class Jigsaw, Random Reporter
Cooperative Base Groups	Students work in long-term (e.g., one semester to several years), heterogeneous, cooperative learning groups with stable membership. Students provide each other with support, encouragement, and assistance to make academic progress. Students meet daily (or when class meets) to provide help and assistance to each other academically and personally.	Student Study Groups
Constructive Controversy	Students are randomly assigned to small groups (e.g., groups of four) and divided into two smaller groups to address different sides of an issue (e.g., global warming exists or does not exist). Each half receives the instructional materials necessary to define their position and point them toward supporting information. Students must reach a consensus on the issue and write a quality group report that synthesizes the best reasoning from both sides.	Students, representing different points of view, working together to reach an agreement

two average spellers, and one advanced speller. Students are responsible for learning their assigned spelling words, but they have their team members to assist and encourage them. Groups earn points based on their team members' performance on weekly spelling tests. Members take responsibility for each other's learning, as well as their own.

Jigsaw—A cooperative group learning method that assigns each of its members a particular learning task. For example, learning about the Civil War may include famous men and women, battles, economic factors, and issues of slavery. Each member chooses a topic and is responsible for teaching his or her team members *all that there is to know* about that topic. Team members meet with members of other groups to form expert groups to discuss and research their topic. For example, the team members of the cooperative groups who chose famous women would meet together in a separate cooperative group focused on learning only about famous women of the Civil War. Following research and discussion, the students return to their own teams and take turns teaching their teammates about their topic. Afterward, students take individual quizzes and earn a team score.

Group Investigation—Similar to the Jigsaw method, except students do not form expert groups. Students work in small groups toward an overall class project. Each group is assigned a different task or activity. Within each group, members decide what information to gather and how to organize and present their findings.

Learning Together—Incorporates heterogeneous student groups that work on a single assignment and receive rewards based on their group product. For example, student groups may be assigned to draw and label the human skeletal system. Each student would receive the same final grade for the group product.

Formal cooperative learning groups differ from traditional learning groups in that most support positive interdependence, individual accountability, group processing, peer responsibility, and heterogeneous membership (Bertucci, Conte, Johnson, and Johnson 2010; Gillies and Boyle 2008; Johnson and Johnson 1999, 2009). Slavin (2014b) states effective cooperative learning requires purposeful grouping of students, interdependent teams of diverse students, a common group goal, and individual accountability and teaches students communication and problem-solving skills. Steps for establishing formal cooperative learning groups include:

1. Identify the objectives for the lesson (academic and social).

2. Decide how to structure the learning groups. This includes deciding on the number of students in each group, how students are assigned to groups, what roles to assign to each student (their management and academic roles), and how to arrange the room.

3. Select and organize the necessary materials.

4. Teach the academic concepts, principles, and strategies the students are to master and apply. Explain the (a) task to be completed, (b) criteria for success, (c) positive interdependence, (d) individual accountability, and (e) expected student behaviors.

5. Model and explicitly teach respectful communication, collaboration, and other desired social skills.

6. Monitor the learning groups' progress, and intervene to provide academic assistance or to address group dynamics when needed.

7. Evaluate student performance against the preset criteria.

Informal cooperative learning includes activities like Think-Pair-Share, Peer Instruction, Whole Class Jigsaw, and Random Reporter (Brame and Biel 2015; Slavin 2014b):

Think-Pair-Share—Students are provided with a question to think about. They can write down their thoughts or think about it silently. When prompted, students turn to a student sitting next to them and discuss their ideas and listen to their partner's ideas. Following their short discussion, students share their thoughts with the whole class.

Peer Instruction—This is similar to Think-Pair-Share except students respond individually to a response system (e.g., Socrative, Kahoot, TurningPoint) before turning to a partner to share their answer. After discussing their response, students have the opportunity to respond again, keeping their answer or selecting another choice. The class responses are then compared and discussed as a whole class.

Whole Class Jigsaw—Students are placed in expert groups to report back what they learned to the whole class. For example, the class may be learning about famous women scientists. The class is divided into small groups, and each group is given the name of a woman scientist. Group members research and learn about their assigned scientist and share what they learned to the whole class.

Random Reporter—Students turn to a partner or work with a small group to discuss a question posed by the teacher. After students decide on a group answer, the teacher randomly calls on students to share their group answer. Teachers can use an app (Random Name Picker, Randomly) or web-based program (e.g., Name Picker Ninja, Random Name Selector), names on popsicle sticks, a spinner, and so on to randomly select students.

As mentioned, informal cooperative learning activities are situations where students work together to achieve a common learning goal in temporary, unplanned groups that last from a few minutes to one class period. Cooperative base groups, on the other hand, are planned groups that are long term (e.g., one semester to several years). One example is study groups, groups that can be implemented at any level, to support students' academic progress and social and emotional growth. The University of Minnesota has designed a student study group program called PAL (Peer Assisted Learning). It is based on the shared characteristics of collaborative learning, cooperative learning groups, and learning communities and offers regularly scheduled, out-of-class sessions facilitated by a fellow student (Arendale 2014). There are variations of the PAL model, including voluntary, mandatory, and co-enrollment. In the co-enrollment model, students earn points toward a course grade for attending. Quantitative and qualitative studies document the academic and personal benefits for students participating in PAL and demonstrate how PAL can help close the achievement gap between students of different ethnicities and levels of academic preparedness (Arendale 2014).

Constructive controversy structures intellectual conflict among students, challenging students to contend with different points of view and come to a consensus or understanding. It helps students develop the following skills for active participation in a democratic society (Sensoy and DiAngelo 2014):

- Engage constructively with alternative perspectives

- Think critically

- Grapple with multiple perspectives

- Build stamina for engaging with new and challenging ideas

- Engage with research

- Raise critical questions

- Tolerate ambiguity

- Recognize the power relations embedded in positionality

- Value collaboration over competition

These skills align with the *Framework for 21st Century Learning* and high-impact educational practices.

Although research supports the use of constructive controversy in face-to-face classes (Johnson and Johnson 2014; Saltarelli and Roseth 2014), researchers report negative effects of using constructive controversy in online, asynchronous discussions. Negative effects include increased competition and conflict, decreased motivation, and reduced academic achievement (Nam 2014; Roseth, Saltarelli, and Glass 2011; Saltarelli and Roseth 2014). Nam (2014) suggests trust-building strategies are more effective than constructive controversy in online, asynchronous cooperative learning environments. Using trust-building strategies can improve students' achievement and *openness and sharing* and *acceptance and support*. Nam (2014) states trust-building strategies require instructors to initiate and maintain trust among group members, monitoring and facilitating trusting behavior. In Nam's study, one group of students was provided with a guideline for learning trust that described five steps for creating a trusting environment: openness, sharing, acceptance, support, and cooperative intentions. The other group received guidelines of developing constructive controversy skills: (1) define controversies as problem-solving situations, (2) be constructively critical of ideas, (3) explore all different points of view, (4) take the point of view or perspective of other members, and (5) negotiate resolutions to students' conflicts in constructing constructive cooperation. Students in the "trust" group felt more positive about online, cooperative learning, and their achievement was significantly higher than the constructive controversy group.

Benefits and Pitfalls of Cooperative Group Learning

Teachers play a significant role in the success of cooperative group learning. When planned, organized, and facilitated appropriately, general findings conclude that:

- cooperative groups are appropriate for any instructional task;

- cooperative groups do just as well or better on achievement than competitive and individualistic learning conditions;

- cooperative conditions appear to work best when students are heterogeneously grouped, although high-ability students do just as well or better in homogeneous groups;

- group discussion promotes higher achievement;

- cooperative learning is more likely to have an effect on student outcomes when cooperation is well defined;

- stereotypes are likely to be reduced when using cooperative groups;

- using cooperative groups promotes equality among perceived ability and leadership roles among males and females;

- cooperative learning can reduce anxiety and create more interesting learning;

- cooperative groups can be more cost-effective than individualistic learning conditions;

- cooperative learning can be effective at all grade levels;

- cooperative learning works best with groups of two to four students. Larger groups make it easier for some students not to contribute. Larger groups (e.g., five to six) may be more appropriate for older, more mature students;

- cooperative conditions can benefit all ability levels;

- cooperative groups support achievement-oriented behavior and healthy social development; and

- cooperative grouping can increase student self-esteem and foster higher-order thinking skills.

Although researchers report many positive outcomes using cooperative learning (Bertucci, Conte, Johnson, and Johnson 2010; Choi, Johnson, and Johnson 2011; Devi, Musthafa, and Gustine 2015; Dietrichson, Bøg, Filges, and Klint Jørgensen 2017; Ebrahim 2012; Slavin 2013, 2014a; Tarhan, Ayyildiz, Ogunc, and Sesen 2013), others note that there are pitfalls (Hall and Buzwell 2013;

Johnson and Johnson 1999; Kao 2013; Kuester and Zentall 2012; Luo 2015; Slavin 1994). Pitfalls include the *free-rider effect* or *social loafing* (members let the more capable members do all the work) and the *sucker effect* (more able members have the less able members do all the work). Social interactive rules, individual accountability, peer evaluation, and grades based on the team's average individual scores can help avoid these pitfalls (Johnson and Johnson 1999; Kao 2013; Lee and Lim 2012; Slavin 1994, 2011). Researchers suggest teacher monitoring, randomly calling on group members to summarize their group's progress or requiring each student to write a concluding summary or a description of his or her group's activity, including a retelling of each individual's role and contribution (Hall and Buzwell 2013; Vermette 1998). Others recommend placing students in smaller groups so it is harder to hide or *free-ride*, define individual expectations of group members, and assign roles that focus on the strengths of the students (Bertucci, Conte, Johnson, and Johnson 2010; Jacobs 2016; Miller, McKissick, Ivy, and Moser 2017). Linnenbrink-Garcia, Rogat, and Koskey (2011) note the importance of affect and social-behavioral engagement in reducing the occurrence of social loafing or the *free-rider* effect. They suggest teaching students to work effectively with peers prior to placing students in groups, helping students develop strategies for alleviating disagreements and disrespectful interactions, and understanding the needs of others. In the case of chronic absenteeism,

- For older students, encourage group members to phone, e-mail, or text peers with what they have missed or post the information to a class group discussion board or private social media site.

- If possible, provide chronically absent students with the opportunity and resources to conduct their work online with their teammates.

- Place chronically absent students in larger groups so that other group members are not as dependent on them.

- Ensure group members have access to the other members' project information and material.

- Structure assessments so group members are not penalized for work missed by the absent student.

- View everyone as a valuable member of the team.

Frequent assessments of a team's progress, including peer evaluations, can help teachers gauge the dynamics of the group. When evaluating team projects, Lee and Lim (2012) found that instructors tend to place greater emphasis on the outcome of the product, whereas students focus on social and managerial competencies (e.g., organizing or coordinating abilities to keep the project moving forward) that the instructor may not easily observe. The researchers stress the importance of peer evaluation, noting "peer evaluation can facilitate the authentic goal of team project-based learning" (222). Expected participation and contributions need to be clarified, and instructors should tell students at the beginning of the project that peer evaluation will be included in the final grade.

How Technology Can Support Collaborative and Cooperative Group Learning

There are numerous ways technology can support collaborative and cooperative group learning. As mentioned, asynchronous online discussion boards can support student communication

Table 2.5. Teacher and Student Activities in the DDD-E Model

Phase	Activities: Teacher	Activities: Students
Decide	Planning • Identify standards and instructional goals. • Decide on project and outline outcomes. • Assess prerequisite skills and knowledge. • Determine assessment techniques. Organizing • Create cooperative groups. • Ensure necessary hardware and software.	• Brainstorm and map content. • Track required tasks. • Conduct research.
Design	• Present design guidelines and templates. • Conduct formative assessment.	• Outline/sequence flowcharts. • Specify design, layout, scripts, and so on.
Develop	• Manage media production. • Facilitate multimedia activities. • Conduct formative assessment.	• Create graphics. • Generate animations. • Produce audio. • Produce video. • Integrate digital elements.
Evaluate	• Provide student assessment. • Reflect on activity and revise for future.	• Debug project. • Evaluate peers. • Conduct self-evaluations.

and the exchange of ideas, and response systems and random name generators can be used to support informal cooperative group instruction. Although constructive controversy strategies may not be best suited for asynchronous environments, researchers report constructive controversy strategies can be used effectively in online, synchronous environments (Roseth, Saltarelli, and Glass 2011; Saltarelli and Roseth 2014). Researchers have also found that Learning Together and STAD computer-assisted instructional strategies can be more effective than individual computer-assisted instruction (Gambari, Yusuf, and Thomas 2015), and mobile learning games can support cooperative learning and increased critical-thinking skills (Lee, Parsons, Kwon, Kim, Petrova, Jeong, and Ryu 2016).

One way technology can be used to support collaborative and cooperative learning in the classroom is through the creation of digital content or multimedia projects. In their book, *Digital Content Creation in Schools*, Ivers and Barron (2015) describe the DDD-E model as a means to help educators effectively design and facilitate cooperative learning groups for digital content creation. DDD-E stands for Decide, Design, Develop, and Evaluate. Teacher and student activities are listed in Table 2.5.

In addition to describing each phase of the DDD-E process, Ivers and Barron (2015) provide alternatives for assigning students to groups (e.g., learning styles, multiple intelligences, student interests) and provide detailed information on alternatives in group size, composition, and structure. Team roles are discussed; teamwork and collaboration are important elements and outcomes of digital projects. Depending on the type of project, members may take on a variety of roles, depending on the type of project. See example roles and projects listed in Table 2.6.

Table 2.6. Potential Team Members

Historical Movie	Public Service Announcement	Online Magazine	Instructional Program
Director	Researcher	Manager	Project manager
Costume designer	Communications manager	Editor	Instructional designer
Scriptwriter	Production	Layout designer	Graphic artist
Production specialist	Editor	Marketing director	Production specialist
Video editor	Distribution	Production specialist	Program author

The team roles need not be independent of each other. In other words, one student may serve as both the costume designer and the script writer. Likewise, students can take turns performing each role and work together for the final product.

As students progress through the various stages of their project, concept mapping tools can help students brainstorm and organize content. A concept map, or mind map, allows students to link concepts and ideas together with words, symbols, or pictures that explain the relationships. Online examples include Mind Maps on GoConqr, Bubbl.us, and MindMup. Apps include Popplet, Simple-Mind+, and MindMeister. Kidspiration and Inspiration are available as desktop- and web-based software, as well as apps. Students can track and share their progress using tools like Google Docs, Evernote, Moodle, Edmodo, and Project Foundry. Flowcharts and storyboards can be created using MS Word, PowerPoint, Google Drawings, Draw.io, SmartDraw, or ClickChart.

During the Develop phase of the DDD-E process, there are numerous free tools that can assist student groups with creating or importing graphics, animations, audio, and video into their projects (see Table 2.7).

Graphics, audio, animation, and video resources can be obtained from searching the Internet too. Some media is public domain (meaning it is free for anyone to use), and some may be royalty free (meaning that someone owns the copyright but allows you to use it with certain restrictions). Many people think everything posted on the Internet is free. It is not. All types of media (e.g., videos, music, documents) are protected by copyright laws, whether it is on the Internet or not. In order to use a graphic or other media element from a web page, you must read the copyright notice on the web page and, if necessary, request permission from the person who created it—especially if it will be used beyond the classroom, including on the Internet. For more information on copyright and fair use, visit the U.S. Copyright Office at https://www.copyright.gov/.

Choosing the appropriate tool for students' projects is important. Depending on students' ability levels, access to technology, time to complete the project, and the goals of the project, teachers may decide to use presentation tools such as PowerPoint, Keynote, Google Slides, or Prezi for collaborative and cooperative projects (Gerido and Curran 2014); website builders such as Weebly, Wix, or Google Sites; or various multimedia creation/writing tools such as Adobe Spark, Book Creator, and Shadow Puppet Edu.

Technology supports collaboration outside of the classroom too. Students can engage with their peers from other countries; work with online experts; and use technology to collaborate on local, regional, national, or global projects. Ideas are discussed in the following chapters.

Table 2.7. Resources for Graphics, Animations, Audio, and Videos

Resource	URL
Clipart • Classroom Clipart • Discovery Education • Pics4Learning	https://classroomclipart.com/ http://school.discoveryeducation.com/clipart/ http://www.pics4learning.com/
Graphics Programs • GIMP • iPiccy • Tux Paint Apps • Adobe Photoshop Sketch • Draw Free • Paper by FiftyThree • Photo Editor by Aviary	https://www.gimp.org/ https://ipiccy.com/ http://www.tuxpaint.org/
Animation Tools and Programs • MonkeyJam • Muvizu • Powtoon • Stykz • Toontastic (also available as an app) Apps • FlipaClip • FrameCast • Puppet Pals HD • Stop Motion Studio • Tellagami	http://monkeyjam.org/ http://www.muvizu.com/ https://www.powtoon.com/ http://www.stykz.net/ https://toontastic.withgoogle.com/
Audio Editors • Audacity • Free Audio Editor • GarageBand (also available as an app) • WavePad (also available as an app)	http://www.audacityteam.org/ https://www.free-audio-editor.com/ https://www.apple.com/mac/garageband/ http://www.nch.com.au/wavepad/index.html
Video Editors • iMovie (also available as an app) • Videolicious (app) • VSDC Free Video Editor • Windows Movie Maker	https://www.apple.com/imovie/ https://videolicious.com/ http://www.videosoftdev.com/ http://www.windows-movie-maker.org/
Audio and Video Clips • C-SPAN Video Library • Educational Video Clips • Find Sounds • Freeplay Music • Library of Congress: Collections with Films, Videos • NASA Videos • National Geographic Video Library • SoundBible.com • SoundEffects+	https://www.c-span.org/about/videoLibrary/ http://www.mrdonn.org/videoclips.html http://www.findsounds.com/ http://freeplaymusic.com/ https://www.loc.gov/film-and-videos/collections/ https://www.nasa.gov/multimedia/videogallery/ http://video.nationalgeographic.com/ http://soundbible.com/ https://www.soundeffectsplus.com/

SUMMARY

Small group instruction and collaborative and cooperative learning activities provide numerous benefits to students and are proven high-impact educational practices. Small group instruction increases student-to-student and teacher-to-student interactions, improves academic achievement, provides better quality and accessibility of instruction, and promotes shared cultural learning. Collaborative and cooperative learning can increase student motivation and engagement; foster social interactions, reduce stereotypes, and create a community of learners; increase students' critical-thinking and problem-solving skills; and provide students with more opportunities for interaction and to consider different points of view—all relevant and meaningful outcomes addressing 21st-century skills.

Technology is an integral part of our 21st-century society. There are numerous ways educators can take advantage of different technology tools to support small group and collaborative and cooperative learning. These include interactive whiteboard apps and other instructional tools to engage students in small instructional groups, record-keeping tools, and online programs to facilitate synchronous small group instruction. Synchronous and asynchronous technologies can be used to support student-led collaborative and cooperative group discussions, student response systems and other technology can help facilitate informal cooperative group instruction, and educators can effectively design and facilitate cooperative learning groups for digital content creation using the DDD-E model.

Small group instruction and collaborative and cooperative learning activities reflect the needs of our global and diverse society. It is important we address the individual needs of our students and provide opportunities for students to work together, solve problems together, plan together, and realize the significance and value of cooperation in our global community.

ACTIVITIES

1. If you are currently teaching in a classroom, discuss how you use small group instruction and manage the rest of the students in the classroom. In what ways do you currently use technology when working with your small groups? Share and compare your experiences with a fellow student or colleague.

2. If you are not currently teaching in a classroom, discuss how you would use small group instruction and manage the rest of the students in the classroom. You might discuss what you have observed in a classroom, what you might do differently, and how technology may assist you. Share and compare your experiences with a fellow student or colleague.

3. In which phases of the CREDE model have you engaged or observed? Share and compare your experiences with a fellow student or colleague. Provide example lessons or activities of the phases you have taught or observed.

4. Work with a partner and find three interactive whiteboard apps to evaluate and compare. In your evaluation, list the names of the apps, how to access them, a brief discussion of each app and its features, and a screenshot of each app, and discuss how the apps are alike and different. Conclude with why you would or would not recommend each app.

5. Think back to a time when you were assigned to work in a collaborative or cooperative group. What was the assignment? What did you enjoy about working with the group? What were some of the challenges? How could your group experience be

improved? How can you apply what you experienced and read in this chapter to creating collaborative or cooperative groups in your classroom? Share and compare your experiences and solutions with a fellow student or colleague.

6. Work with two other students and become an *expert* on one of the graphics programs, animation tools and programs, audio editors, or video editors. (Make sure student groups do not choose the same program!) Share your expertise with the class by providing a brief overview of the tool, a demonstration of the program, and a handout or resources that support learning the program.

7. In a group of three or four, complete the Ch2. Resource Page: Sample Lessons at the end of this chapter.

8. Digital content creation supports creativity and innovation, critical thinking and problem solving, and communication and collaboration—important 21st-century skills. For this activity, place yourself into a group of three or four and decide on a topic to teach. Your team will teach this topic by using a video editing program or an animation tool. Identify who will be the lead designer, programmer, writer, videographer, prop coordinator, choreographer, music director, researcher, and so on. Roles will vary, depending upon your project. Members can share roles, but members should be designated as leads to ensure tasks are completed. You will have a credit screen at the end of your production (product) that lists your members and their roles, as well as any other credits necessary (e.g., thanks for the use of Jose's kitchen, music credits). Follow the DDD-E model presented in the Ch2. Resource Page: DDD-E Project at the end of this chapter.

9. Work with two or three other people to create a unit where the culminating product is a cooperative group multimedia project that demonstrates student learning. Use the DDD-E model to guide your planning and student activities. Decide on the standards, goals, and best tools for the project; how students will be grouped; student roles; timeline for the unit, and so on. Include all of the necessary instructional materials. Identify the International Society for Technology in Education's (ISTE) technology standards that will be addressed, and discuss the necessary modifications and accommodations you will make to ensure all of your students can succeed.

10. Identify two technology resources not identified in this chapter that can be used to support collaborative assignments and projects. Share these with your peers.

RESOURCE LIST

Apps

Concept mapping tools: Popplet, SimpleMind+, and MindMeister

Interactive whiteboards: ShowMe, Jot!, BaiBoard, Educreations Interactive Whiteboard

Multimedia writing tools: Book Creator, Shadow Puppet Edu

Random name generators: Random Name Picker, Randomly

Record keeping: Evernote, Google Keep

Coding Sites

Alice: http://www.alice.org/

Code.org: https://code.org

Made with Code: https://www.madewithcode.com/

Collaborative Work Environments

Edmodo: https://www.edmodo.com/

Evernote: https://evernote.com/

Google Docs: https://www.google.com/docs/about/

Moodle: https://moodle.com/

Project Foundry: http://www.projectfoundry.com/

Concept Mapping Tools

Bubble.us: https://bubbl.us/

Inspiration: http://www.inspiration.com/

Kidspiration: http://www.inspiration.com/Kidspiration

Mind Maps: https://www.goconqr.com/en/mind-maps/

MindMup: https://www.mindmup.com/

Copyright

U.S. Copyright Office: https://www.copyright.gov/

Create Storyboards and Flowcharts

ClickChart: http://www.nchsoftware.com/chart/index.html

Draw.io: https://www.draw.io/

Google Drawings: https://docs.google.com/drawings/

Microsoft PowerPoint: https://www.microsoft.com/

Microsoft Word: https://www.microsoft.com/

SmartDraw: https://www.smartdraw.com/

Graphics, Animations, Audio, and Video Tools

Adobe Spark: https://spark.adobe.com/

(For further resources, see Table 2.7.)

Online Conferencing, Discussion, and Chat

Skype: https://www.skype.com/

VoiceThread: https://voicethread.com/

Zoom: https://zoom.us/

Presentation Tools

Google Slides: https://www.google.com/slides/about/

Keynote: https://www.apple.com/keynote/

Microsoft PowerPoint: https://www.microsoft.com/

Prezi: https://prezi.com/

Random Name Generator

Name Picker Ninja: https://namepickerninja.com/

Random Name Selector: https://www.teachstarter.com/widget/random-name-selector/

Website Builders

Google Sites: https://sites.google.com/

Weebly: https://www.weebly.com/

Wix: https://www.wix.com/

REFERENCES

Arendale, D. 2014. Understanding the peer assisted learning model: Student study groups in challenging college courses. *International Journal of Higher Education*, 3(2), 1–12.

Beaulieu-Jones, L. and Proctor, C. 2016. A blueprint for implementing small-group collaborative discussions. *Reading Teacher*, 69(6), 677–682.

Behfar, K., Mannix, E., Peterson, R., and Trochim, W. 2011. Conflict in small groups: The meaning and consequences of process conflict. *Small Group Research*, 42(2), 127–176.

Bertucci, A., Conte, S., Johnson, D. W., and Johnson, R. T. 2010. The impact of size of cooperative group on achievement, social support, and self-esteem. *Journal of General Psychology*, *137*(3), 256–272.

Brame, C. J. and Biel, R. 2015. Setting up and facilitating group work: Using cooperative learning groups effectively [online]. Available at http://cft.vanderbilt.edu/guides-sub-pages/setting-up -and-facilitating-group-work-using-cooperative-learning-groups-effectively/. Accessed on September 29, 2017.

BrckaLorenz, A., Garvey, J. C., Hurtado, S. S., and Latopolski, K. 2017. High-impact practices and student-faculty interactions for gender-variant students. *Journal of Diversity in Higher Education*, *10*(4), 350–365.

Bruffee, K. A. 1995. Sharing our toys: Cooperative learning versus collaborative learning. *Change: The Magazine of Higher Learning*, *27*(1), 12–18.

Chambers, B., Slavin, R. E., Madden, N. A., Abrami, P., Logan, M. K., and Gifford, R. 2011. Small-group, computer-assisted tutoring to improve reading outcomes for struggling first and second graders. *Elementary School Journal*, *111*(4), 625–640.

Choi, J., Johnson, D. W., and Johnson, R. T. 2011. Relationships among cooperative learning experiences, social interdependence, children's aggression, victimization, and prosocial behaviors. *Journal of Applied Social Psychology*, *41*(4), 976–1003.

Coffey, G. 2012. Literacy and technology: Integrating technology with small group, peer-led discussions of literature. *International Electronic Journal of Elementary Education*, *4*(2), 395–405.

Comer, D. and Lenaghan, J. 2013. Enhancing discussions in the asynchronous online classroom: The lack of face-to-face interaction does not lessen the lesson. *Journal of Management Education*, *37*(2), 261–294.

Cross, R., Rebele, R., and Grant, A. 2016. Collaborative overload. *Harvard Business Review* [online]. Available at: https://hbr.org/2016/01/collaborative-overload. Accessed on January 13, 2018.

Day, D. and Kroon, S. 2010. "Online literature circles rock!" Organizing online literature circles in a middle school classroom. *Middle School Journal*, *42*(2), 18–28.

Devi, A. P., Musthafa, B., and Gustine, G. G. 2015. Using cooperative learning in teaching critical thinking in reading. *English Review: Journal of English Education*, *4*(1), 1–14.

Dietrichson, J., Bøg, M., Filges, T., and Klint Jørgensen, A. 2017. Academic interventions for elementary and middle school students with low socioeconomic status. *Review of Educational Research*, *87*(2), 243–282.

Ebrahim, A. 2012. The effect of cooperative learning strategies on elementary students' science achievement and social skills in Kuwait. *International Journal of Science and Mathematics Education*, *10*(2), 293–314.

Gambari, A. G., Yusuf, M. O., and Thomas, D. A. 2015. Effects of computer-assisted STAD, LTM and ICI cooperative learning strategies on Nigerian secondary school students' achievement, gender and motivation in physics. *Malaysian Online Journal of Educational Science*, *3*(4), 11–26.

Gerido, L. and Curran, M. C. 2014. Enhancing science instruction through student-created PowerPoint presentations. *American Biology Teacher*, *76*(9), 627–631.

Gillies, R. M. and Boyle, M. 2008. Teachers' discourse during cooperative learning and their perceptions of this pedagogical practice. *Teaching and Teacher Education: An International Journal of Research and Studies*, *24*(5), 1333–1348.

Hall, D. and Buzwell, S. 2013. The problem of free-riding in group projects: Looking beyond social loafing as reason for non-contribution. *Active Learning in Higher Education, 14*(1), 37–49.

Hollo, A. and Hirn, R. G. 2015. Teacher and student behaviors in the contexts of grade level and instructional grouping. *Preventing School Failure, 59*(1), 30–39.

Hossain, M. A., Tarmizi, R. A., and Ayud, A. F. M. 2012. Collaborative and cooperative learning in Malaysian mathematics education. *Indonesian Mathematical Society Journal on Mathematics Education, 3*(2), 103–114.

Ivers, K. S. and Barron, A. E. 2015. *Digital content creation in schools.* Santa Barbara, CA: ABC-CLIO.

Jacobs, G. M. 2015. Collaborative learning or cooperative learning? The name is not important; Flexibility is. *Beyond Words, 3*(1), 32–52.

Jacobs, G. M. 2016. Ten strengths of how teachers do cooperative learning. *Beyond Words, 4*(1), 10–16.

Järvelä, S. Järvenoja, H., Malmberg, J., Isohätälä, J., and Sobocinski, M. 2016. How do types of interaction and phases of self-regulated learning set a stage for collaborative engagement? *Learning and Instruction, 43*, 39–51.

Johnson, D. W. and Johnson R. T. 1999. Making cooperative learning work. *Theory into Practice, 38*(2), 67–73.

Johnson, D. W. and Johnson, R. T. 2009. An educational psychology success story: Social interdependence theory and cooperative learning. *Educational Researcher, 38*, 365–379.

Johnson, D. W. and Johnson, R. T. 2014. Cooperative learning in 21st century. *Anales De PsicologíA/ Annals of Psychology, 30*(3), 841–851.

Kao, G. 2013. Enhancing the quality of peer review by reducing student 'free riding': Peer assessment with positive interdependence. *British Journal of Educational Technology, 44*(1), 112–124.

Kruse, L. G., Spencer, T. D., Olszewski, A., and Goldstein, H. 2015. Small groups, big gains: Efficacy of a tier 2 phonological awareness intervention with preschoolers with early literacy deficits. *American Journal of Speech-Language Pathology (Online), 24*(2), 189–205.

Kuester, D. A. and Zentall, S. S. 2012. Social interaction rules in cooperative learning groups for students at risk for ADHD. *Journal of Experimental Education, 80*(1), 69–95.

Küster, M. 2016. Writing beyond the letter. *Tijdschrift Voor Mediageschiedenis, 19*(2), 1–17.

Laal, M. and Ghodsi, S. M. 2012. Benefits of collaborative learning. *Procedia—Social and Behavioral Sciences, 31*, 486–490.

Ledford, J. R. and Wolery, M. 2015. Observational learning of academic and social behaviors during small-group direct instruction. *Exceptional Children, 81*(3), 272–291.

Lee, H. and Lim, C. 2012. Peer evaluation in blended team project-based learning: What do students find important? *Educational Technology & Society, 15*(4), 214–224.

Lee, H., Parsons, D., Kwon, G., Kim, J., Petrova, K., Jeong, E., and Ryu, H. 2016. Cooperation begins: Encouraging critical thinking skills through cooperative reciprocity using a mobile learning game. *Computers & Education, 97*, 97–115.

Linnenbrink-Garcia, L., Rogat, T. K., and Koskey, K. L. K. 2011. Affect and engagement during small group instruction. *Contemporary Educational Psychology, 36*(1), 13–24.

Luo, Y. 2015. Design fixation and cooperative learning in elementary engineering design project: A case study. *International Electronic Journal of Elementary Education, 8*(1), 133–146.

McInnerney, J. M. and Roberts, T. S. 2005. Collaborative and cooperative learning. In C. Howard, J. V. Boettcher, and L. Justice (Eds.), *Encyclopedia of distance learning* (Vol. 1, pp. 269–276). Hershey, PA: Idea Group Reference.

Miller, N., McKissick, B., Ivy, J., and Moser, K. 2017. Supporting diverse young adolescents: Cooperative grouping in inclusive middle-level settings. *Clearing House: A Journal of Educational Strategies, Issues and Ideas, 90*(3), 86–92.

Nam, C. W. 2014. The effects of trust and constructive controversy on student achievement and attitude in online cooperative learning environments. *Computers in Human Behavior, 37*, 237–248.

Nam, C. W. and Zellner, R. D. 2011. The relative effects of positive interdependence and group processing on student achievement and attitude in online cooperative learning. *Computers & Education, 56*(3), 680–688.

OECD. 2015. *Students, computers and learning: Making the connection.* PISA, OECD Publishing, Paris [online]. Available at: http://dx.doi.org/10.1787/9789264239555-en. Accessed on May 14, 2018.

Quebec Fuentes, S. 2013. Small-group discourse: Establishing a communication-rich classroom. *The Clearing House: A Journal of Educational Strategies, Issues and Ideas, 86*(3), 93–98.

Rockwood, H. S., III. 1995a. Cooperative and collaborative learning. *National Teaching & Learning Forum, 4*(6), 8–9.

Rockwood, H. S., III. 1995b. Cooperative and collaborative learning. *National Teaching & Learning Forum, 5*(1), 8–10.

Roseth, C. J., Saltarelli, A. J., and Glass, C. R. 2011. Effects of face-to-face and computer-mediated constructive controversy on social interdependence, motivation, and achievement. *Journal of Educational Psychology, 103*(4), 804–820.

Saltarelli, A. J. and Roseth, C. J. 2014. Effects of synchronicity and belongingness on face-to-face and computer-mediated constructive controversy. *Journal of Educational Psychology, 106*(4), 946–960.

Sensoy, Ö. and DiAngelo, R. 2014. Respect differences? Challenging the common guidelines in social justice education. *Democracy & Education, 22*(2), 1–10.

Slavin, R. E. 1994. *Cooperative learning: Theory, research, and practice* (2nd ed.). Needham Heights, MA: Allyn & Bacon.

Slavin, R. E. 1999. Comprehensive approaches to cooperative learning. *Theory into Practice, 38*(2), 74–79.

Slavin, R. E. 2011. *Educational psychology theory and practice* (10th ed.). Boston, MA: Pearson Education, Inc.

Slavin, R. E. 2013. Effective programmes in reading and mathematics: Lessons from the Best Evidence Encyclopaedia. *School Effectiveness & School Improvement, 24*(4), 383–391.

Slavin, R. E. 2014a. Cooperative learning and academic achievement: Why does groupwork work? *Anales De PsicologíA, 30*(3), 785–791.

Slavin, R. E. 2014b. Making cooperative learning powerful. *Educational Leadership, 72*(2), 22–26.

Tarhan, L., Ayyildiz, Y., Ogunc, A., and Sesen, B. A. 2013. A jigsaw cooperative learning application in elementary science and technology lessons: Physical and chemical changes. *Research in Science & Technological Education, 31*(2), 184–203.

Tomasello, M. 2016. Cultural learning redux. *Child Development, 87*(3), 643–653.

Vermette, P. J. 1998. *Making cooperative learning work: Student teams in K–12 classrooms.* Upper Saddle River, NJ: Prentice-Hall.

Wallhead, T. and Dyson, B. 2017. A didactic analysis of content development during cooperative learning in primary physical education. *European Physical Education Review, 23*(3), 311–326.

Wasik, B. 2008. When fewer is more: Small groups in early childhood classrooms. *Early Childhood Education Journal, 35*(6), 515–521.

Wyatt, T. and Chapman-DeSousa, B. 2017. Teaching as interaction: Challenges in transitioning teachers' instruction to small groups. *Early Childhood Education Journal, 45*(1), 61–70.

Ch2. Resource Page: Sample Lessons

View the following videos for sample lesson ideas and approaches.
https://youtu.be/—SnKiYGYJE
(real world with puppet—video and iMovie or similar)
https://youtu.be/JCq1XFDVZA4
(created with Powtoon: https://www.powtoon.com/)
https://youtu.be/AHyLqPspWR0
(real world rap example—video and iMovie or similar)
https://youtu.be/zy3r1zlC_IU
(stop motion approach)

After viewing the videos, discuss and compare each approach and lesson, what did and did not make it affective, and what you would do differently. Find two more short videos online (five minutes or less) that you believe would be appropriate for teaching your students a specific topic. Provide the URLs and a brief description of each video for class discussion.

DECIDE

1. Decide on a topic to teach. Identify the standard and grade level.

2. Decide on the tool you will use to create the product. The product should be posted to YouTube and be three to five minutes long.

3. Identify your roles within the group.

4. Set goals and create a timeline of when to accomplish each goal.

5. Decide how you will evaluate each of your group member's participation. Create the evaluation (peer evaluation). (E)

DESIGN

6. Construct storyboards, flowcharts, and/or scripts to organize and plan the product.

7. Gather props, graphics, music, devices, and so on that may be needed.

8. Check progress against timeline and make notes about group members' participation. (E)

DEVELOP

9. Rehearse or create a beta version to test/proof your work.

10. Record/save/post your final product.

11. Evaluate your work on the basis of your original goals. (E)

(E)VALUATE

12. Evaluation takes place throughout each step.

13. Share your lesson with your classmates. Groups provide each other with constructive feedback.

Project Tips:

1. Review the project guidelines and instructions (see Activity #8). Focus on the content, clarity, and delivery of your lesson. Choose a multimedia tool that you are comfortable with or has a low learning curve (e.g., iMovie, Windows Movie Maker). If you or someone in your group has advanced technology skills, feel free to be adventurous. Else, remember that there is a limited amount of time to complete this project. Create a timeline of due dates!

2. Remember to follow copyright and fair use laws. Give credit where credit is due, and use works (e.g., music) that are original or in the public domain.

3. Include a "credit" screen at the end of your production (product) that lists your members and their roles, as well as any other credits necessary.

4. Arrange set times to meet so that each team member is able to participate in the production. Plan ahead!

Day of the Presentation:

1. Make sure your video is accessible and ready to view. Have a backup plan (video saved on drive, disc, etc.)

2. Begin your presentation with a brief discussion of your DDD-E process.
   a. Share how you identified your topic, team roles, and tool. Identify your grade level and standard, as well as anything else you would like us to know about your target audience.
   b. Provide examples of your storyboards or other materials of your planning stage.
   c. Discuss the development process—what went well, issues, and so on.

3. Provide a brief introduction to your video and show it.

4. Discuss the overall challenges, learning experience, and what you would do differently (if anything) next time.

5. Presentations should be roughly 10–15 minutes, including video.

6. Team members should complete and submit a peer evaluation of their group members and themselves.

PROJECT RUBRIC

Criteria	5–4	3–2	1–0
Content	Overall, the content is clear, accurate, and appropriate for the intended audience.	The content is somewhat clear, but it is still appropriate for the intended audience.	The content is not clear, is inaccurate, or is not appropriate for the intended audience.
Spelling, Punctuation, Grammar, and Tech Glitches	The content is professionally presented with no spelling, punctuation, or grammar errors.	The content contains several spelling, punctuation, and grammar errors, but it is still easy to follow.	The content contains numerous spelling, punctuation, and grammar errors, or it is difficult to follow because of tech glitches.
Credit	The project credits the members of the team and borrowed sources.	Not all credits are provided.	No credits are provided.
Originality, Engagement, and Quality	The project is original and engaging. The quality of the presentation is professional.	The project is similar to others, but it is still engaging. The quality of the presentation is good.	The project is similar to others and is not engaging or looks like it was thrown together at the last minute.
Assignment Guidelines	The project follows the provided guidelines and instructions.	The project follows most of the provided guidelines and instructions.	The project does not follow most of the provided guidelines or instructions.

Group and Self-Evaluation

Submit the following:

1. Your name and name of group members.

2. Your team's strengths.

3. Your team's weaknesses.

4. What you learned about yourself in the process of working with others.

5. What you would do differently next time you worked as a team.

6. Your contributions to the team.

7. On a scale of 1 to 5 (5 being the highest), how would you rate your contribution to the team?

8. On a scale of 1 to 5 (5 being the highest), how would you rate your team member's(s) contribution to the team? (Provide the name and rating for each team member.)

Chapter 3

Social Competence, Culturally Responsive Teaching, and Inclusive Classrooms

OVERVIEW

Social competence, culturally responsive teaching, and inclusive classrooms are intertwined. In order to build students' social competence, teachers need to provide students with opportunities to grow socially, emotionally, and cognitively. This requires *teaching to and through* students' cultural diversity, developing social consciousness and individual self-worth using culturally responsive teaching (Gay 2013). Developing social competence requires students to examine how stereotypes, the media, and institutionalized norms can impact their attitudes and perceptions of others too. Creating just, equitable, and inclusive learning environments allows teachers to expand students' understanding of the similarities and differences among people. Diversity is what empowers us, giving us the ability to learn from other perspectives and see the world beyond our own limitations.

This chapter begins by discussing how students' social competence is relevant to their success in today's global society. Examples of how technology can help build students' social competence are provided. Next, the significance of culturally responsive teaching is addressed, including the importance of meeting students' individual needs and learning styles. Characteristics of culturally responsive teachers are examined, and Howard Gardner's Theory of Multiple Intelligences is presented. Strategies, resources, and instructional ideas of how technology can support culturally responsive teaching are offered. Lastly, issues regarding the importance of establishing a just, equitable, and inclusive learning environment are examined. Universal Design for Learning (UDL) is discussed, and the importance of eliminating gender inequities, stereotypes, and bias toward marginalized groups is presented. In addition, how the media perpetuates stereotypes is investigated. Multiple resources are provided to help teachers learn more about marginalized groups, as well as strategies for maintaining a just, equitable, and inclusive learning environment.

SOCIAL COMPETENCE

Social competence refers to the "social, emotional, and cognitive skills and behaviors that children need for successful social adaptation" (Social Competence 2016, 1105). It is the ability to interact effectively with people different from one's self in order to achieve shared goals, as well as one's personal and professional goals. Social competence is critical in today's workforce. For example, despite workers' STEM (science, technology, engineering, and mathematics) skills, Google reports its most successful employees are good coaches, communicate and listen well, possess insights into others (including different values and points of view), have empathy toward and are supportive of their coworkers, are critical thinkers and problem solvers, and can make connections across complex ideas (Strauss 2017).

People from different cultures may express social competence differently. For example, Han and Thomas (2010) discuss the differences of high-context and low-context cultures. In high-context cultures, social identity and group interests are more valued, as are assertiveness, leadership, and verbal expression. Withdrawn behavior is viewed upon negatively. In low-context cultures, individual identity and personal interests are more valued, as are compliance, respectfulness, and subtle cues. Withdrawn behavior is preferred over aggressive behavior. In addition, there are different expectations among cultures regarding greetings (e.g., bowing, handshaking, hugging, and kissing), eye contact, and so on (Allen and Steed 2016).

In order to become socially competent, students need experiences learning about, working with, and interacting effectively with people from various cultures and backgrounds. Researchers suggest that social engagement and play are the foundation to young students' development of social competence (Daniel, Santos, Peceguina, and Vaughn 2015; Fung and Cheng 2017) and developing diverse friendships supports cultural socialization (Tran, Lee, and Zárate 2011). Students can develop social competence through collaborative and cooperative group activities, learning communities, and social media (Johnson and Johnson 2014; Vossen and Valkenburg 2016). Working together, students learn how differences combine to make meaning.

Ensuring students are socially competent in today's interconnected, global society requires students to understand and respect others different from themselves (Partnership for 21st Century Learning 2007). Students who lack social competence are more likely to experience social anxiety and engage in reactive aggression (Kaeppler and Erath 2017; Robinson, Fetterman, Hopkins, and Krishnakumar 2013). Educators can support the development of students' social competence by providing a culturally responsive and inclusive learning environment.

How Technology Can Help Build Students' Social Competence

Technology easily connects people via social media, websites, and cell phones. Teachers can use online environments to actively engage students in discussion forums, wikis, and other online resources to help students construct knowledge and learn more about each other in the classroom. Koutamanis, Vossen, Peter, and Valkenburg (2013) state online communication can have a positive effect on offline social competence. Asynchronous communication provides students time to compose their thoughts, have an opportunity to be heard without being interrupted, and have more opportunities for interaction and to consider different points of view (Coffey 2012; Comer and Lenaghan 2013). Educators can build online learning communities that focus on curricular topics or create classroom *get to know me* activities. For example, students can use Web tools, apps, and presentation programs, such as Weebly, Wix, ShowMe, PowerPoint, Google Slides, Google Sites, Adobe Spark, and Book Creator to create and share multimedia résumés or posters of their interests, family traditions, favorite things, and so on. They can also take advantage of digital storytelling, which combines the art of telling stories with the use of multimedia, including graphics, audio, video, and Web publishing (see http://digitalstorytelling.coe.uh.edu/). Creating digital stories involves eight steps:

1. Decide on an idea or topic, and write a proposal.

2. Research and learn more about the topic.

3. Write the script for the story.

4. Design and sequence the storyboards for the project.

5. Gather and create the multimedia elements needed for the project (e.g., audio, video, and graphics).

6. Develop the project.

7. Share the project.

8. Get feedback and reflect.

Applying this process to creating *All About Me* stories, students may:

1. brainstorm about the facts they want to share about themselves (this can be done as a whole class to generate a variety of ideas from which to choose);

2. research and learn more about the chosen facts (e.g., family history);

3. outline and write a script for their story;

4. design and sequence the storyboards for the project;

5. gather and create the multimedia elements needed for the project;

6. develop the project;

7. share the project; and compare and contrast students' stories, looking at similarities and what makes them unique.

Students may create digital stories in groups of two or three, also, allowing them to more intimately learn about each other's differences and similarities. They can conclude their project with what they learned about each other.

In situations where students are in predominately homogenous environments, the Internet provides opportunities for students to engage and collaborate with others different from themselves. Sometimes these students are just a community away. Educators can look for schools with different demographics than their own by using Ed-Data (https://www.ed-data.org/) and contacting teachers via the school website who may be interested in collaborative activities. Additional resources that help teachers connect are listed in Table 3.1.

Additional resources for global projects are presented in Chapter 4. Teachers can use Google Docs, Moodle, Edmodo, and other shared spaces to support student collaboration across schools (see Chapter 2). Students can record themselves and introduce each other by using tools like Screencast-O-Matic and Screencastify (screen/webcam recording tools), Zoom, VoiceThread, or video apps on their smartphones. Technology provides students with more opportunities to interact with and learn about others different from themselves, helping to build students' social competence and 21st-century skills.

CULTURALLY RESPONSIVE TEACHING

Every child brings his or her uniqueness to the classroom, creating a diverse classroom environment. These unique characteristics include students' linguistic, race, socioeconomic, gender, ability, and religious differences. Despite students' differences, they have much in common—the desire to learn, be valued, have fun, and succeed (Wall 2017). Each student's pathway to success, however, is different. Gay (2013) advocates educators teaching to and through students' cultural diversity using culturally responsive teaching, a pedagogical approach that develops social

Table 3.1. Resources That Help Teachers Connect with Other Teachers

Resource	URL	Description
Google Hangouts for Teachers	https://sites.google.com/a/lsr7.net/hangoutsforteachers/home	Google's free videoconferencing tool that is available for teachers to use as part of Google Apps for Education.
Google+ Educational Technology Community	https://plus.google.com/communities/117916783328771901842	One of the many educational community sites on Google+.
Staffrm	https://staffrm.io/	A web-based community for teachers.
TeachersConnect	http://www.teachersconnect.com/	A smartphone app that allows teachers to share ideas and collaborate with other teachers through group discussions, community posts, and private messages.
Twitter (via Edutopia)	https://www.edutopia.org/blog/twitter-expanding-pln	A list of education-related Twitter chats created by Edutopia.

consciousness and individual self-worth by incorporating cultural knowledge about different groups in all subjects and skills taught. Gay (2010, 31) defines culturally responsive teaching as "using cultural knowledge, prior experiences, frames of reference, and performance styles of ethnically diverse students to make learning encounters more relevant to and effective for them." Culturally responsive teachers have several characteristics (Adkins 2012; Elliot-Engel and Westfall-Rudd 2016; Ladson-Billings 2009; Lynch 2014; Rychly and Graves 2012).

- They set high expectations for all learners and believe all students can succeed.

- They are empathetic, caring, and knowledgeable about different cultures.

- They maintain a positive perspective on parents and families.

- They see themselves as part of the community and giving back to the community.

- They help students make connections to their local, national, racial, cultural, and global identities.

- They build fluid and equitable relationships with students that extend beyond the classroom.

- They develop a community of learners and foster collaboration, acting as a facilitator of instruction rather than someone who delivers instruction.

- They provide a student-centered and culturally mediated instruction.

- They celebrate diversity of language and provide instructional materials to non-native speakers tailored to their level of English fluency, as well as in their primary language, and encourage students to master English.

- They encourage critical thinking and questioning.

- They build bridges and use scaffolding to develop students' knowledge.

- They provide real-world learning opportunities, making meaningful connections between school and real-life situations.

- They reflect upon their own beliefs about people from other cultures and their own cultural frame of reference.

Culturally responsive teachers need to be reflective about their own cultural backgrounds, biases, and assumptions too. They need to reflect upon their own cultural frame of reference when interpreting people from other cultures. Weinstein, Tomlinson-Clark, and Curran (2004, 29) explain that "by bringing our implicit, unexamined cultural biases to a conscious level, we are less likely to misinterpret the behaviors of our culturally different students and treat them equitably." Implicit biases affect our opinions, behaviors, interactions, and attitudes toward others in an unconscious way (Gay 2010). Without first examining their own biases and values, teachers may go into a classroom with a preconceived idea of how students should respond and learn on the basis of the teacher's own life experiences, beliefs, and feelings (Lambeth and Smith 2016). All students will not succeed if teachers structure their classrooms to conform to themselves and not to their students. Educators need to adjust their pedagogical approaches to meet the diverse needs of their students.

In order to meet the diverse needs of their students, teachers need to learn about their students. This includes students' linguistic background; academic abilities; learning styles; physical, social, and emotional development; cultural and family background; health issues; interests, and so on. Teachers should be familiar with the students' community and home life too. Learning about students' personal, social, and academic needs helps educators customize their instruction and teaching strategies. Teachers can match their teaching strategies to their students' learning styles or *intelligence* by providing students with multiple options for demonstrating mastery of academic content (Gay 2013).

Howard Gardner's Theory of Multiple Intelligences

Students are diverse in many ways, including how they learn. Culturally responsive teachers recognize the uniqueness of their students and provide learning opportunities that align with and strengthen their students' identities and natural ways of learning (Gay 2013; Rychly and Graves 2012). Researchers suggest that students have several ways of learning or *multiple intelligences* (Gardner 1983, 1999, 2006, 2011a; Samples 1992; Sternberg 1994). Perhaps the most recognized theory of multiple intelligences is Howard Gardner's Theory of Multiple Intelligences (Gardner 1983, 1999, 2011a). Gardner defines intelligence as "a biopsychological potential to process information that can be activated in a cultural setting to solve problems or create products that are of value in a culture" (Gardner 1999, 33–34). He suggests that intelligences are neural conditions that will or will not be activated by opportunities, personal decisions, or values. He also states that everyone possesses these intelligences, noting that people acquire and represent knowledge in different ways. Gardner's proposed eight areas of intelligence are as follows:

1. Linguistic Intelligence: The ability to use words effectively, whether orally or in writing.

2. Logical-Mathematical Intelligence: The capacity to use numbers effectively and to reason well.

3. Spatial Intelligence: The ability to perceive the visual-spatial world accurately and to perform transformations on those perceptions.

4. Bodily-Kinesthetic Intelligence: Expertise in using one's body to express ideas and feelings and facility in using one's hands to produce or transform things.

5. Musical Intelligence: The ability to perceive, discriminate, transform, and express musical forms.

6. Interpersonal Intelligence: The ability to perceive and make distinctions in the moods, intentions, motivations, and feelings of other people.

7. Intrapersonal Intelligence: Self-knowledge and the ability to act on the basis of that knowledge.

8. Naturalist Intelligence: Expertise in recognizing and classifying living and nonliving forms within one's environment. Gardner (1999, 49) notes, "The young child who can readily discriminate among plants or birds or dinosaurs is drawing on the same skills (or intelligence) when she classifies sneakers, cars, sound systems, or marbles."

Gardner identified these intelligences on the basis of a series of tests that included eight different criteria. Gardner has speculated on the possibility of a ninth intelligence, existential intelligence, noting that there is suggestive evidence that it exists (Gardner 2011a). He has also explored the idea of a pedagogical intelligence, as well as considered a digital intelligence (Gardner 2011a). Additional intelligences have been proposed—including spirituality, moral sensibility, sexuality, humor, intuition, and creativity—but it remains to be seen whether these proposed intelligences meet the required criteria (Armstrong 2009; Gardner 1999, 2011a). Howard Gardner can be seen and heard on YouTube (see https://youtu.be/oY2C4YgXm7I) discussing his theory of multiple intelligences.

There are several important elements to remember about Gardner's Theory of Multiple Intelligences. Armstrong (2009) states that

- each person possesses all eight intelligences;

- most people can develop each intelligence to an adequate level of competency;

- intelligences usually work together in complex ways; and

- there are many ways to be intelligent within each category.

Many educators have successfully implemented Gardner's Theory of Multiple Intelligences into their classrooms (Dorfman and Rosenberg 2013; Douglas, Burton, and Reese-Durham 2008; Eksi 2009; Gardner 2011b; Kukovec 2014; La Porte 2016; Vermonden and Alcock 2013). Applying Gardner's Theory of Multiple Intelligences can benefit all learners, including students with learning disabilities, gifted students, second-language learners, and students from diverse cultural backgrounds (Dorfman and Rosenberg 2013; Hernández-Torrano, Ferrándiz, Ferrando, Prieto, and Del Carmen Fernández 2014; La Porte 2016; Perez and Beltran 2008). Gardner's Theory of Multiple Intelligences supports interdisciplinary teaching too (Kukovec 2014).

Although it is important for culturally responsive teachers to provide students with multiple options to demonstrate mastery and to build upon their different intelligences, Dweck (2007) emphasizes the importance of not praising students' intelligence, abilities, or traits (person praise). She states that this creates a *fixed mindset*. Students with a fixed mindset focus on how smart they are and pursue tasks that confirm their intelligence, avoiding activities that do not. According to

Dweck, this minimizes students' desire to learn and causes negative consequences when students face challenges beyond what they think they can do. Person praise can cause students to feel ashamed and helpless when they fail (Brummelman et al. 2014; Skipper and Douglas 2012). Researchers suggest praising and acknowledging students' efforts (Brummelman et al. 2014; Dweck 2007). This creates a *growth mindset*: the belief that effort improves learning and skills and that intelligence is not fixed. Studies show praising students' efforts (process praise) can increase students' motivation, self-efficacy, and achievement (Brummelman et al. 2014; Dweck 2007; Kamins and Dweck 1999).

Culturally responsive classroom practices include the teaching of social skills, providing students with opportunities to explore and learn more about individual differences as well as similarities. Classroom material (e.g., books, pictures, video, and software) should represent culturally diverse children and families. Stereotypes should be challenged, and every effort should be made to ensure an equitable and inclusive learning environment.

How Technology Can Support Culturally Responsive Teaching

Technology provides students with multiple ways to demonstrate mastery of academic content. Students can choose tools that provide them with the opportunity to express themselves through words, pictures, video, audio, or a combination of different media. When assigning cooperative groups to create digital content, teachers can utilize students' strengths by assigning students tasks on the basis of their intelligences (Ivers and Barron 2014). See Table 3.2.

Teachers can use technology to assess their own and their students' multiple intelligences. Table 3.3 provides resources for assessing multiple intelligences.

Technology can be used to help teachers learn more about their students in other ways, too. Teachers can create online surveys using websites like SurveyPlanet or SurveyMonkey and learn more about their students through ePortfolios created with tools like Kidblog, PortfolioGen, and Weebly.

Technology can be used to provide real-world learning opportunities for students, helping them make meaningful connections between school and real-life situations. For example, cooperative groups can create digital presentations, websites, videos, professional brochures, or pamphlets based upon what they learn about a local community issue. Student groups can conduct research and connect with real-world experts via the Internet. Students can share their findings to create community awareness, as well as present possible solutions for solving the issue. Projects can be conducted as a whole class, too, broken into expert groups (e.g., Whole Class Jigsaw). Examples of student-led projects include the following:

> Students learn about soil bacteria through creating multimedia information pamphlets. They consult professional microbiologists and cartoonists, conduct original research, and then distribute their completed pamphlets to local garden centers, universities, and flower shops. (Curtis 2001)
>
> Students gain insight into the advertising industry as well as gain an understanding of a range of elements linked to chocolate production and consumption. Students investigate how advertising affects our desire for a product and how to make effective branding and advertising. Students visit a cocoa production plant and get marketing advice from people in the industry. Students present their documentary at a film festival at the local cinema. (The Chocolate Project 2017)

Table 3.2. Roles of Multiple Intelligence in Digital Content Creation

Intelligence	Observed Student Behaviors	Leadership Roles in Digital Content Creation
Linguistic	Loves to read books, write, and tell stories; good memory for names, dates, and trivia; communicates well	Gather and develop text for project; provide narration; keep journal of group progress
Logical-Mathematical	Excels in math; has strong problem-solving skills; enjoys playing strategy games and working on logic puzzles	Design flowchart; write scripting and programming code; develop navigation routes
Spatial	Needs a mental or physical picture to best understand things; draws figures that are advanced for age; doodles a lot	Create graphics, animation, and other visual media for project; design layout and storyboards
Body-Kinesthetic	Excels in one or more sports; good fine-motor skills; tendency to move around, touch things, and gesture	Keyboard information; operate multimedia equipment; organize storyboards based on flowchart; gather offline resources and information
Musical	Remembers melodies; recognizes when music is off-key; has a good singing voice; plays an instrument; hums a lot	Identify works for content integration; create musical score for project; input audio/sound effects
Interpersonal	Enjoys socializing with peers; has leadership skills; has good sense of empathy and concern for others	Coordinate group efforts; help set group goals; help solve group disputes
Intrapersonal	Has strong sense of self; is confident; prefers working alone; has high self-esteem; displays independence	Conduct independent research to share with teammates; pilot test multimedia projects; lead multimedia presentations
Naturalist	Enjoys the outdoors, plants, and animals; easily recognizes and classifies things within his/her environment	Collect outside elements for incorporation into projects; organize project work

Resource personnel from the Solid Waste Authority or Department of Natural Resources visit the classroom and make a presentation on the importance of taking care of the environment. They bring examples of products made from recycled goods to show students that you can reuse items to create something new and to get students excited about inventing their own product. Students collaborate and discover ways to use recycled items. Students create a new product using at least 50% recycled materials. Students present their product and the process they used to create it though a multimedia presentation. (Trash to Treasure n.d.)

Technology can be used to help students reflect upon their own beliefs about people from other cultures and their own cultural frame of reference. In addition to global learning projects

Table 3.3. Resources for Assessing Multiple Intelligences

Resource	URL	Description
Child Development Institute: Multiple Intelligences	https://childdevelopmentinfo.com/learning/multiple_intelligences/#.WeEQCltSzlU	A list of questions for adults and observation questions about their children.
Edutopia Multiple Intelligence Self-Assessment	https://www.edutopia.org/multiple-intelligences-assessment	An online, 24-question quiz that takes less than five minutes to complete.
LoveToKnow: Multiple Intelligence Test for Children	http://kids.lovetoknow.com/wiki/Multiple_Intelligence_Test_for_Children	Printable multiple intelligence test for children.
Multiple Intelligences for Adult Literacy and Education	http://www.literacynet.org/mi/assessment/findyourstrengths.html	An online, 56-question questionnaire, provided by Dr. Terry Armstrong.
Niall Douglas: Multiple Intelligence Test	http://www.nedprod.com/Niall_stuff/intelligence_test.html	An online multiple intelligence test available in multiple languages via Google Translate.

(discussed in more detail in Chapter 4) and learning about each other through class projects, students can use resources on the Internet to learn more about different cultures and people's lives. For example, teachers can help students connect with others who are different from them by partnering with other classrooms (see "How Technology Can Help Build Students' Social Competence" mentioned earlier). Teachers can create lessons that incorporate the Global Lives Project, a video library of life experiences from people around the world (see http://globallives.org/). National Geographic provides numerous resources and lessons that focus on cultural awareness. For example, Cultural Identity of the Lost Boys (see https://www.nationalgeographic.org/activity/cultural-identity-lost-boys/) is a lesson that uses excerpts from *God Grew Tired of Us* to help students recognize the importance of culture and how cultures are similar and different. The Teaching Channel showcases "Exploring Emigration: Cultural Identity," based on *The Lost Boys*, also (see https://www.teachingchannel.org/videos/teaching-cultural-identity). Cooperative groups can create digital documentaries about an assigned culture and present their findings back to the class, school, or community. In addition to the Global Lives Project, students may incorporate video files, music, and other media that helps them demonstrate what they have learned about their assigned culture. Clarke, DeNora, and Vuoskoski (2015) suggest that listening to music of an unfamiliar culture can have a positive effect on cultural attitudes. Tables 3.4 and 3.5 provide lists of resources that can help students (and teachers) learn more about different cultures.

Additional technology tools and resources that can support culturally responsive teachers are translation programs (see Table 3.6). Wearable translation devices are available too. These include ili (a wearable device that hangs around your neck and translates speech in real-time) and the Pilot (two earpieces, one for each speaker, providing real-time translation). More devices are on the horizon.

Table 3.4. Resources for Learning about Different Cultures

Resource	URL	Description
AMP Global Youth	https://ampglobalyouth.org/students/learn-about-different-cultures/	Offers information and opportunities to learn more about different cultures and world events.
Commisceo Global: Country and Culture Guides	http://www.commisceo-global.com/country-guides	Provides cultural information on over 80 countries, including language, society, culture, food, beliefs, business practices, and social etiquettes.
Global Lives Project	http://globallives.org/	A video library of life experiences from people around the world.
Kwintessential	http://www.kwintessential.co.uk/resources/guides/	A language service site that also provides country guides and profiles.
Mama Lisa's World: International Music and Culture	http://www.mamalisa.com/	Songs, rhymes, recipes, videos, and more from around the world.
My Learning	http://www.mylearning.org/	An eclectic assortment of free learning resources from arts, cultural, and heritage organizations.
National Geographic: Education	https://www.nationalgeographic.org/education/	Provides numerous activities, resources, and lesson plans for teachers, including learning about different cultures.
Radio Garden	http://radio.garden/	An interactive site where students can listen to radio stations from all over the world.
Teaching Channel	https://www.teachingchannel.org/	Includes an online community for teachers, as well as videos, activities, and resources searchable by topic, subject, and grade level.
YouTube	https://youtu.be/QLISC-opl0Y https://youtu.be/JChxT9Yv2iw https://youtu.be/YKyRbyRhMnw	YouTube videos demonstrating how greetings, emotions, and gestures differ across cultures.

Table 3.5. Resources for Learning about Different Cultural Holidays

Resource	URL	Description
Christmas around the World	https://www.whychristmas.com/cultures/	Students learn how Christmas is celebrated in different countries. Hanukkah and Kwanzaa are discussed too.
Education World: Holidays around the World lesson plans	http://www.educationworld.com/a_lesson/lesson213.shtml	Lesson plans and resources for December celebrations and observances from several cultures.
Holiday and Observances around the World	https://www.timeanddate.com/holidays/	Provides the date, holiday name, and holiday type, as well as information about the holiday, for numerous countries throughout the world.
Scholastic Holiday Sampler	https://www.scholastic.com/teachers/articles/teaching-content/holidays-sampler-around-world/	Provides a variety of resources and lesson plans for different holidays throughout the world.

Table 3.6. Translation Websites and Apps

Resource	URL	Description
Google Translate	https://translate.google.com/ (also available as an App)	Translates over 100 different languages. App includes offline translation support for over 50 languages, speech-to-speech translation, picture translation, and more.
iTranslate Voice	App	Provides text-to-speech and voice-to-voice translation. Supports 44 languages and dialects.
Microsoft Translator	App	Translates over 60 different languages and provides speech recognition and real-time conversation mode for some languages.
Papago	App	Translates Korean, Japanese, and Mandarin to and from English. When there's more than one possible way to translate a word or a phrase, Papago asks users to choose between two different images to establish context. Includes currency converter.
SayHi	App	Offers speech-to-speech translation in 90 languages and dialects. Some languages are text only.
SpanishDict	http://www.spanishdict.com/	Provides English/Spanish translation and other resources for learning Spanish.
TextGrabber	App	Optical Character Recognition app that "reads" text from images and offers translations.
Waygo	App	Uses camera to translate Chinese, Japanese, and Korean characters with no data connection required.

JUST, EQUITABLE, AND INCLUSIVE EDUCATION

Culturally responsive teaching helps to ensure just, equitable, and inclusive learning environments, as does UDL. UDL is a set of principles for curriculum development that reinforces the importance of customizing and adjusting instruction for individual needs. Some of the key components of UDL curriculum are as follows (National Center on Universal Design for Learning 2014):

- *Goals* acknowledge the different needs of learners and are separated from means. Teachers can provide more options and alternatives (e.g., varied pathways, tools, strategies, and scaffolds) for reaching mastery. Curriculum focuses on developing *expert learners.*

- *Methods* are evidence based and change depending on the goals of instruction. They are flexible and varied, based on the needs of individual learners, the purpose of the task, learners' social/emotional abilities, and the classroom climate.

- *Materials* include multiple media and just-in-time supports such as hyperlinked glossaries and background information; tools and supports needed to access, analyze, organize, synthesize, and demonstrate understanding in varied ways; and alternative pathways to success, including choice of content where appropriate, varied levels of support and challenge, and options for maintaining interest and motivation.

- *Assessment* focuses on the goals, not the means. By broadening means to meet the needs of individual learners, UDL assessments more accurately measure learner knowledge, skills, and engagement.

UDL lessons are designed with all students' needs in mind. Instruction and content are delivered in multiple ways to address students' various learning styles, students can present what they know in different ways, and students are provided with multiple opportunities for engagement. UDL is especially beneficial for students with learning disabilities and behavioral disorders in the general education classroom (Johnson-Harris and Mundschenk 2014). UDL also supports the affective and academic needs of English language learners (Rao and Torres 2017). Resources for learning more about UDL include the Center for Applied Special Technology (http://www.cast.org/) and the National Center on Universal Design for Learning (http://www.udlcenter.org/).

Learning about students is a critical component of just, equitable, and inclusive classrooms. Teachers need to be aware of students' cognitive, culture, and emotional background, as well as their home life. Teachers may encounter students who come from very impoverished environments, moving from place-to-place as their parents struggle to find work. This can lead to learning gaps in their education, as well as feelings of insecurity, low self-esteem, and inadequacy (Walker et al. 2013). Teachers often stereotype impoverished students as lazy, unmotivated, and unintelligent and believe that their parents do not care about education (Ullucci and Howard 2015). Steps teachers can take to provide a more just, equitable, and inclusive environment include minimizing or eliminating fees and providing supplemental support for the cost of supplies and field trips; ensuring students have access to free meals and medical support offered by the school and community sponsors; providing access to computers, books, and other learning materials; and focusing on students' internal assets rather than their external possessions or appearance.

Just, equitable, and inclusive classrooms support students' culture, linguistic needs, learning styles, access, and abilities, as well as strive to eliminate gender inequities, stereotypes, and bias toward marginalized groups. Although some progress has been made in the United States (e.g., women can vote, desegregation was implemented, and same-sex couples have the right to marry), there remains a tremendous amount of inequity and discrimination. For example, researchers report that women earn considerably less than men, and racial discrimination in the workplace still exists (Brown and Patton 2017; Hegewisch, Phil, and Williams-Baron 2017; Mohr and Purdie-Vaughns 2015). Racial discrimination and injustice exist outside of the workplace, too. Social movements continue to bring awareness to the injustice and inequity experienced by non-White groups. Discrimination and injustice are prevalent among those who identify as LGBTQ+ too. For example, in some states, teachers are not allowed to talk about LGBTQ+ topics or promote LGBTQ+ as a positive lifestyle (GLSEN 2017; Segal 2017). As we progress into the 21st century, social stigmas, stereotypes, and injustice remain (Joseph, Viesca, and Bianco 2016; La Macchia, Louis, Hornsey, Thai, and Barlow 2016; Pietri, Johnson, and Ozgumus 2017).

Using the words of Nelson Mandela, "Education is the most powerful weapon you can use to change the world." Educators can foster learning environments that are just, equitable, and inclusive and help students challenge stereotypes. Educators can provide students with an inclusive curriculum, small group learning opportunities with peers different than themselves, positive representations of people different than themselves, media literacy skills (see Chapter 6), and opportunities to *walk in other people's shoes*. Service-learning opportunities and project-based learning (see Chapter 5) can help students gain new perspectives and understandings of those different than themselves, as can technology. For example, using virtual reality simulations, researchers have found that users who see themselves in the body of a different race result in significant reductions of the levels of implicit bias against that racial group (Hasler, Spanlang, and Slater 2017; Maister, Slater, Sanchez-Vives, and Tsakiris 2015).

Changing the world takes educators who are committed against racism, discrimination, and stereotypes. Teachers need to ensure every child sees himself or herself as equal and capable. One way educators can help female students challenge the stereotypes associated with STEM fields is addressing the effects that societal beliefs and learning environments have on girls' interests and achievements in STEM. According to Hill, Corbett, and Rose (2010), girls' achievement in STEM increases when teachers and parents

- tell girls that their intelligence expands with experience and learning. This helps girls create a growth mindset;

- remind girls that boys and girls are equally capable in the STEM fields; and

- provide opportunities for girls to work on spatial skills.

Teachers and parents must address their own implicit bias too. Research suggests that STEM fields can be perceived as masculine, and women in STEM fields are judged less likeable and competent than men (Hill, Corbett, and Rose 2010; Makarova and Herzog 2015).

Research suggests that society initiates student failure and adversity by imposing gender guidelines and norms (Al-Attar, De Meyer, El-Gibaly, Michielsen, Animosa, and Mmari 2017; Basu, Zuo, Lou, Acharya, and Lundgren 2017; Blum, Mmari, and Moreau 2017; Yu et al. 2017). For example, *a woman's place is in the home* and *big boys don't cry* are institutionalized norms, created by a dominate group in society (Ridgeway 2009). Gender is what society deems appropriate for males and females and may differ by culture. Sex is biologically determined. Gender is a social construct; hence, children's choice of clothes, toys, colors, and so on is not something that is hardwired into their brains (Fine 2010). In fact, the color pink (a *girl* color) was originally associated with boys, and the color blue (a *boy* color) was once thought to be more appropriate for girls (Eliot 2009). Gender norms and inequality are created, perpetuated, and reinforced through early childhood experiences, socialization, and the media (Collins 2011; Popa and Gavriliu 2015).

How the Media Perpetuates Stereotypes

The media plays an influential role on how viewers perceive gender, race, ethnicity, poverty, persons with disabilities, and LGBTQ+ individuals, contributing to stereotypes, bias, and unfavorable perceptions (Bullock, Wyche, and Williams 2001; Bussey and Bandura 1999; Shrum, Wyer, and O'Guinn 1998; Tukachinsky 2015; Tukachinsky, Mastro, and Yarchi 2017; Ward and Aubrey 2017). On prime-time television, women (of all races) are underrepresented and sexualized, with White women more likely to be seen as the victim of crimes (Collins 2011; Parrott and Parrott 2015b; Ward and Aubrey 2017). White men dominate the media and are typically portrayed as heroes, successful, intelligent, and leaders (Martins and Harrison 2012; Ward and Aubrey 2017). Blacks are typically featured in sitcoms or crime dramas where they are often depicted as unprofessional, criminals, or aggressors; Latinos are seen as criminals, subservient, or intellectually inept; Asian and Native Americans are almost invisible on mainstream media; and Black and Latina women are portrayed as hypersexual and less professional (Martins and Harrison 2012; Tukachinsky, Mastro, and Yarchi 2017). When depicted, Asians are often portrayed as kung fu masters, cunning, successful financially, technology-savvy, and *foreign* (Sun, Liberman, Butler, Lee, and Webb 2015). Of the top 100 movies of 2015, 32 percent of the movies depicted a female as the lead; only three female leads/coleads were played by female actors from an underrepresented racial/ethnic group; women were more than three times as likely as their male counterparts to be shown in sexually revealing clothing; 73.7 percent of characters were White; 12.2 percent Black; 5.3 percent Latino; 3.9 percent Asian; < 1 percent Middle Eastern, American Indian/Alaskan Native, or Native Hawaiian/Pacific Islander; and 3.6 percent other or mixed race; only 14 of the movies depicted an underrepresented lead or colead, and none of these were Asian; 17 percent of films did not feature one Black or African American speaking or named character on screen; Asian characters were missing across 49 films; there were no LGBTQ+ identified as leads or coleads; 82 of the top 100 movies of 2015 did not depict one LGBTQ+ speaking or named character; 40 percent of LGBTQ+ characters were from an underrepresented racial/ethnic group; only two lesbian parents were portrayed; and only 2.4 percent of all speaking or named characters were shown with a disability (Smith, Choueiti, and Pieper 2016).

People with disabilities are rarely represented in the media, but Wohl (2017) reports people with disabilities are less frequently portrayed negatively when compared to past decades. He states that advertisements, television, and movies include people with physical and intellectual disabilities "not simply as a means of emphasizing their differences or 'specialness,' but as part of an effort to more accurately represent our society's diversity" (Wohl 2017, 22). Unfortunately, Wohl notes the majority of actors playing these roles are not disabled even though over 2,000 actors self-identify as having a disability.

Although there are more positive portrayals of people with disabilities than in the past, there remain many adverse depictions of and jokes about people with disabilities, reinforcing negative stereotypes. People with mental illness are typically characterized as dangerous, violent, and criminals; people with communicative disorders are often portrayed in a comedic role, having weak social or mental skills, or being unhappy; and prime-time cartoons frequently exaggerate and mock characters with disabilities (Evans and Williams 2015; Parrott and Parrott 2015a; Wohl 2017). Individuals are alienated, isolated, ridiculed, and bullied as a result of having a mental or physical disability.

Representation of LGBTQ+ individuals in the media is limited, but researchers claim there has been positive progress as the result of some celebrities *stepping out of the closet* (Kelso 2015; Nölke 2018). Stereotypes still exist, however, including portraying gay men as White, preoccupied with body issues, overtly effeminate, flamboyant, foolish, and usually from upper-middle class, while lesbians are hypersexualized (Mclaughlin and Rodriguez 2017; Nölke 2018). Non-White

LGBTQ+ individuals are rarely represented, adding to what researchers call triple oppression: oppression by society in general, by the respective ethnic group, and by the racism of the White LGBTQ+ population (Nölke 2018).

Media's portrayal of people in poverty is often negative and degrading, perpetuating social stigmas and exclusion (Hamilton et al. 2014). Stereotypes include portraying impoverished people as lazy, uneducated, drug addicts, criminals, and ineffective parents (Bullock, Wyche, and Williams 2001; Hamilton et al. 2014). Poverty is portrayed as a choice or as a result of not trying, not as a result of divorce, separation, death, illness, or disability, leaving people in severe economic circumstances; societal inequities; part-time employment; or limited work options as a result of caring responsibilities (Chase and Walker 2013). Social success is often defined in terms of financial gains and material possessions, often making impoverished adults and children feel insecure, unwelcomed, and flawed; have low-self-esteem; and see themselves as failures (Walker et al. 2013). Chase and Walker (2013, 740) report that people in poverty feel shame and shamed by society, noting that shame is co-constructed, "combining an internal judgement of one's own inabilities; an anticipated assessment of how one will be judged by others; and the actual verbal or symbolic gestures of others who consider, or are deemed to consider, themselves to be socially and/or morally superior to the person sensing shame."

Stereotypes and inequity exist in media targeting children. Researchers report boys outnumber girls in children's programming, boys are more often the protagonist, girls are valued by their physical attractiveness, boys are the providers and leaders, and relationships are heterosexual (Kirsch and Murnen 2015; Martin 2017; Ward and Aubrey 2017). Other perpetuating stereotypes that exist in children programming include the idea that female beauty is linked to thinness and male attractiveness is linked to being physically fit (Simpson, Kwitowski, Boutte, Gow, and Mazzeo 2016). Non-White character depictions in children's entertainment often reinforce racist stereotypes and can have negative effects on children's self-efficacy and self-esteem (Martins and Harrison 2012; Williams and Korn 2017).

The impact media can have on children is alarming. In addition to reinforcing racist stereotypes, Golden and Jacoby (2017) discuss how Disney Princess media perpetuates and reinforces gendered stereotypes in young children, increasing girls' focus on their beauty, clothing and accessories, and specific body movements. According to the researchers, this sets the groundwork for self-objectification and puts girls at the risk of developing a limited understanding of femininity, leading to depression, anxiety, and eating disorders. LGBTQ+, or what Kelso (2015) refers to as *gender-creative children*, have very limited role models in the media. Kelso (2015, 1082) suggests, "Gender-creative children who spend a lot of time with television could very well internalize its predominantly gender-normative and heteronormative outlook, perhaps eventually learning to regard themselves as misfits."

Being aware of the forces that shape students' attitudes and perceptions outside of the classroom is just as important as knowing how the classroom environment and curriculum materials impact students' learning, self-identity, and respect for others. Creating a just, equitable, and inclusive environment includes culturally responsive teaching and proactively taking steps to ensure classroom resources and activities are inclusive and do not reinforce stereotypes. Teachers must be aware of their feedback to students, being careful not to perpetuate and strengthen stereotypical expectations for females (e.g., you look beautiful) and males (e.g., you are so strong and brave). Stereotypes are the first step in stigmatization, informing attitudes and future prejudicial behavior in the real world (Link and Phelan 2014). Educators should have high expectations of all of their students and be mindful not to label or alienate students who may not *fit* within the teachers' own norms. Just, equitable, and inclusive environments are gender neutral. There are not boy lines and girl lines; activities include girls and boys both playing with cars, blocks, dolls, and playhouses; and girls and boys are capable of succeeding in all subjects. Teachers of just, equitable, and inclusive environments believe humanity, not possessions, determines success. Teachers use process praise rather than personal praise, helping to create a growth mindset in each of their students. As educators prepare students for the needs of the 21st century, global workforce, all students need the opportunity to succeed and be valued.

How Technology Can Support Just, Equitable, and Inclusive Classrooms

Creating just, equitable, and inclusive classrooms is part of being a culturally responsive educator. Culturally responsive teaching includes incorporating cultural knowledge about different groups in all subjects and skills taught. Technology supports teachers in creating just, equitable, and inclusive learning environments by providing access to resources that might not otherwise be available. For example, there are numerous websites that discuss the historical contributions of women, Blacks, Latinos, and other marginalized groups (see Tables 3.7 and 3.8). Teachers can use the Internet to contact role models and guest speakers who represent the students in their classroom. Students can create digital projects that identify, discuss, and celebrate who they consider a hero from their own culture.

While race is unique to select groups, identifying as LGBTQ+ or having physical or mental disabilities crosses all racial groups. Individuals who identify as LGBTQ+, however, not only suffer the social stigma, prejudice, and discrimination of the public in general but can also be shunned, demeaned, and rejected by their own family (Page 2017; Permenter 2012). This can lead to homelessness, substance abuse, and suicide (Figueiredo and Abreu 2015; Page 2017; Su et al. 2016).

Table 3.7. Resources for Learning More about Women's Contributions

Resource	URL	Description
Biography Online: Women Who Changed the World	http://www.biographyonline.net/people/women-who-changed-world.html	A list of famous influential women, including women's rights activists, poets, musicians, politicians, humanitarians, and scientists. There are lists specific to female athletes, authors, and others too.
HistoryNet: Famous Women in History	http://www.historynet.com/famous-women-in-history	Information, timelines, resources, and articles about famous women in history.
National Women's Hall of Fame	https://www.womenofthehall.org/	Pictures, biographies, and videos of accomplished American women.
Time: 50 Women Who Made American Political History	http://time.com/4551817/50-women-political-history/	Pictures and brief biographies of women in American political history.
Women in World History	http://www.womeninworldhistory.com/	Pictures, biographies, lesson and unit plans, and video documentaries of famous women throughout history, including women rulers.

Table 3.8. Resources for Learning More about Contributions from Other Marginalized Groups

Resource	URL	Description
Biography Online: Groups	https://www.biography.com/people/groups	Information about various groups of people (e.g., including those specific to different ethnic groups).
Disabled World: Well-Known People with Disabilities	https://www.disabled-world.com/artman/publish/article_0060.shtml	An extensive list with brief biographies of famous people with disabilities, organized by specific disabilities.
Famous and Inspirational LGBT People	http://www.lgbthistorymonth.org.uk/history/LGBTpeople.htm	Biographies of famous LGBTQ+ people in history, the arts, entertainment, politics, and more.
Gold Sea: The Most Inspiring Asian Americans of All Time	http://goldsea.com/Personalities/Inspiring/inspiring.html	Information about the achievements of 130 Asian Americans.
PBS: Black Culture Connection	http://www.pbs.org/black-culture/home/	Information, videos, and other instructional resources on the contributions and history of Black Americans.
USA People Search: Famous Hispanics in History	https://articles.usa-people-search.com/content-famous-hispanics-in-history.aspx	An extensive list with brief descriptions of famous Hispanics in history.

In today's world, homophobia still exists, similar to racism, with the exception that the penalty for having a gay or lesbian relationship in some countries is imprisonment or death (Carroll and Mendos 2017). There are resources on the Web that can help educators better understand the needs of LGBTQ+ students and learn how to address the bias and discrimination these students encounter within and outside of their own racial groups (see Table 3.9).

Numerous websites provided information, lesson plans, and resources for addressing discrimination and prejudice in general. These include the following:

- Breaking the Prejudice Habit (http://breakingprejudice.org/)

- Partners against Hate (http://www.partnersagainsthate.org/)

- Teaching Tolerance (https://www.tolerance.org/)

- Understanding Prejudice (http://www.understandingprejudice.org/)

There is a plethora of resources on the Internet to help teachers create just, equitable, and inclusive learning environments, as well as help students understand the negative consequences of prejudice, discrimination, and stereotypes. Technology provides educators and students with access to current and essential educational resources and multifaceted learning tools.

Assistive technologies are learning tools designed to support students with disabilities. They help students with disabilities utilize their strengths and work around their challenges, helping to

Table 3.9. LGBTQ+ Educational Resources

Resource	URL	Description
APA LGBT Resources and Publications	http://www.apa.org/pi/lgbt/resources/	Resources for addressing bias and discrimination, learning more about LGBTQ+, and more.
FAIR Education Website	http://www.faireducationact.com/	Lesson plans and resources for an inclusive curriculum.
Gay, Lesbian, and Straight Education Network	https://www.glsen.org/	Educator guides; inclusive curriculum support; lesson plans on bullying, bias, and diversity; and more.
Out Alliance	http://www.gayalliance.org/	LGBTQ+ education, resources, speakers, inclusive curriculum, and more.
PBS: Teacher's Guide to LGBT Youth Resources	http://www.pbs.org/newshour/extra/2015/06/teachers-guide-to-lgbt-youth-resources/	Numerous links to LGBTQ+ resources, including a state-by-state resource list.

provide a just, equitable, and inclusive learning environment. Assistive technologies include the following:

- *Text-to-speech programs*—Students can see and hear text at the same time.

- *Screen readers*—Similar to text-to-speech programs, but they can also read system icons, menu bars, and more. Some screen readers can output to Braille.

- *Speech/voice recognition software*—Students can verbalize commands and can have the task completed by the device.

- *Word prediction software*—Provides a list of predicted words while the student is trying to type.

- *Display or magnification software*—Enlarges images on the screen for visually impaired students.

Many of these assistive technologies exist on devices people use every day, enhancing their communication experiences. Assistive technology includes specialized hardware, also, such as alternative keyboards and other input devices (e.g., trackballs, joysticks, touch pads, switches, and pointing devices) and output devices such as specialized monitors and Braille embossers. Braille embossers are used to produce raised Braille dots on paper. There are many resources on the Web to help teachers (and parents) learn more about different disabilities and assistive technologies (see Table 3.10).

Just, equitable, and inclusive classrooms are safe environments for all students. In addition to supporting students' many learning needs, just, equitable, and inclusive learning environments strive to eliminate stereotypes, bias, and discrimination. This includes confronting and eliminating bullying. Cyberbullying, a digital form of bullying, can exist anywhere people view or share digital content. This makes it easier to bully or harass others, as well as remain anonymous. Technology can support teachers' efforts to address bullying and cyberbullying. Information, resources, and lessons can be found on numerous websites (see Table 3.11).

Table 3.10. Resources for Learning More about Students with Disabilities

Resource	URL	Description
Edutopia: Assistive Technology: Resource Roundup	https://www.edutopia.org/article/assistive-technology-resources	Videos and list of assistive technology resources.
National Center on Accessible Educational Materials	http://aem.cast.org/	Information, resources, and policies regarding accessible materials.
PBS Parents: Learning Disabilities	http://www.pbs.org/parents/education/learning-disabilities/	Information about different types of disabilities and how to support children who have them.
Reading Rockets: Assistive Technology for Kids with Learning Disabilities: An Overview	http://www.readingrockets.org/article/assistive-technology-kids-learning-disabilities-overview	An article about assistive technology with links to additional resources.
Understood: For Learning and Attention Issues	https://www.understood.org/	Multiple categories for learning more about learning and attention issues, assistive technologies, resources, and more.

Table 3.11. Antibullying Resources

Resource	URL	Description
Common Sense Media: Cyberbullying, Haters, and Trolls	https://www.commonsensemedia.org/cyberbullying#	FAQs, articles, and videos about cyberbullying.
Cyberbully	http://cyberbully.org/	Teacher, parent, student guides, and more.
Cyberbullying Research Center	https://cyberbullying.org/	Resources and information for educators, parents, and students, as well as a family Internet use contract.
NSTeens: Cyberbullying	http://www.nsteens.org/videos/cyberbullying	Video stories from teens about cyberbullying.
StopBullying.gov	https://www.stopbullying.gov/	Information, resources, laws, prevention tips, and more about bullying and cyberbullying.

Table 3.12. Resources for Technology Donations and Grants

Resource	URL	Description
Computers for Learning	https://computersforlearning.gov/	Free computer equipment from federal agencies.
Computers with Causes	http://www.computerswithcauses.org/application.htm	Provides computer donations to individuals and organizations with computer needs.
Digital Wish	http://www.digitalwish.com/dw/digitalwish/teachers	Funding and grant support and other technology resources.
Donors Choose	https://www.donorschoose.org/teachers	Manages donor contributions to posted teacher's projects.
National Cristina Foundation	https://www.cristina.org/become-partner/	Provides technology donations to qualified organizations that engage in the education; rehabilitation; or training of people with disabilities, at-risk students, or economically disadvantaged persons.

Various digital technologies can help students and teachers learn more about cultures and life experiences different from their own. Technology provides students with opportunities to learn from and work collaboratively with others representing diverse cultures, religions, and lifestyles. Equitable access to technology remains an issue, however. Disadvantaged students are less likely to have computers with Internet access at home. In the United States, the difference between advantaged and disadvantaged students' access at home is almost 20 percent (OECD 2015). Teachers need to consider students' technology access when assigning digital projects. It is possible that students' only access to computers is in the classroom. In classrooms where access to computers is limited, teachers can find support via the Internet (see Table 3.12).

SUMMARY

Social competence is critical for today's diverse, globally connected world. Educators can build students' social competence by creating classroom environments that foster learning about, working with, and interacting effectively with people from various cultures and backgrounds. Culturally responsive teaching addresses the unique needs of culturally diverse students and incorporates cultural knowledge about different groups in all subjects and skills taught. Culturally responsive teachers set high expectations for all learners and believe all students can succeed, develop a community of learners and foster collaboration, and reflect upon their own beliefs about people from other cultures and their own cultural frame of reference. In addition, they provide students with multiple options for demonstrating mastery of academic content and match their teaching styles to students' learning style.

Culturally responsive teaching takes place in just, equitable, and inclusive learning environments. Just, equitable, and inclusive learning environments are necessary to build students' social competence. Just, equitable, and inclusive learning environments include UDL and strive to eliminate gender inequities, stereotypes, and bias toward marginalized groups. Discrimination and inequities remain prevalent in today's society, and stereotypes continue to be perpetuated through media.

There are many ways technology can be used to support teachers in their efforts to increase students' social competence; engage in culturally responsive teaching; and create just, equitable, and inclusive learning environments. Technology supports opportunities for students to interact with and learn more about students within and outside of their classroom, work collaboratively with 21st-century tools, express their knowledge in different ways, focus on their strengths, and access resources to further their knowledge and understanding of people different from themselves. The Internet provides numerous resources to support just, equitable, and inclusive learning environments and help students and teachers understand the negative consequences of prejudice, discrimination, and stereotypes.

ACTIVITIES

1. People from different cultures may express social competence differently. Think about your own culture and decide whether you think it reflects a high-context culture or a low-context culture, as described by Han and Thomas (2010). Share your reflection and rationale with a fellow student or colleague.

2. Using a technology tool of your choice, create an *All About Me* digital story. See the Ch3. Resource Page: All About Me at the end of this chapter.

3. Taking the implicit bias test at https://implicit.harvard.edu. Reflect upon and share your results with a partner.

4. In what ways are you a culturally responsive teacher? Share with your classmates or a colleague the characteristics you possess that align with the characteristics of a culturally responsive teacher. Share how you would like to improve your ability to be a culturally responsive teacher too.

5. Work with a partner and share how you can learn more about students' linguistic background; academic abilities; learning styles; physical, social, and emotional development; cultural and family background; health issues; interests; community; and home life.

6. Complete the multiple intelligences test at http://www.literacynet.org/mi/assessment/findyourstrengths.html

    a. Take a screenshot, print, or save a copy of your results.

    b. In a small group, discuss (a) what you believe are your own multiple intelligence strengths and weaknesses and how these support or don't support how you feel you learn best and (b) how your own learning style and personal beliefs may impact your teaching.

7. Use the Ch3. Resource Page: GEG to explore how greetings, emotions, and gestures differ across cultures.

8. Create a team with two or three additional students, and select one of the following groups. Each team should have a different group. Complete the activities described on the Ch3. Resource Page: Media Project 1.

    a. People with disabilities

    b. LGBTQ+ individuals

    c. Females

    d. Non-White males

    e. Low socioeconomic-status individuals

9. Create a team with two or three additional students. Complete the activities described on Ch3. Resource Page: Media Project 2.

10. Work with one or two people to create a digital story about a person who was born poor and became known for their achievements and contributions. See the Ch3. Resource Page: Born Poor.

11. Brainstorm a list of technology resources at your school or at a school you have observed. Share and compare your list with a partner. Discuss what you know about your students' home access to technology tools. Discuss how this impacts or will impact your teaching and what steps you can take to improve your students' access to technology.

12. Identify two technology resources not identified in this chapter that can be used to support social competence, culturally responsive teaching, and inclusive classrooms. Share these with your peers.

RESOURCE LIST

Antibullying Resources

See Table 3.11.

Collaborative Work Environments

Edmodo: https://www.edmodo.com/

Google Docs: https://www.google.com/docs/about/

Moodle: https://moodle.com/

Educational Uses of Digital Storytelling

Digital Storytelling: http://digitalstorytelling.coe.uh.edu

ePortfolio Tools

Kidblog: https://kidblog.org/

Portfolio Gen: https://www.portfoliogen.com/

Weebly: https://www.weebly.com/

Implicit Bias Test

Project Implicit: https://implicit.harvard.edu

Internet Resources for Learning More about Different Cultures and People's Lives

Cultural Identity of the Lost Boys: https://www.nationalgeographic.org/activity/cultural-identity-lost-boys/

Exploring Emigration: Cultural Identity: https://www.teachingchannel.org/videos/teaching-cultural-identity

The Global Lives Project: http://globallives.org/

(For further resources, see Tables 3.4 and 3.5.)

LGBTQ+ Educational Resources

See Table 3.9

Online Survey Tools

SurveyMonkey: https://www.surveymonkey.com/

SurveyPlanet: https://surveyplanet.com/

Resources for Addressing Discrimination and Prejudice

Breaking the Prejudice Habit: http://breakingprejudice.org/

Partners against Hate: http://www.partnersagainsthate.org/

Teaching Tolerance: https://www.tolerance.org/

Understanding Prejudice: http://www.understandingprejudice.org/

Resources for Learning More about and Connecting with Different Schools

Ed-Data: https://www.ed-data.org/

(For further resources, see Table 3.1.)

Resources for Learning More about Students with Disabilities

See Table 3.10.

Resources for Technology Donations and Grants

See Table 3.12.

Screen/Webcam Recording Programs

Screencastify: https://www.screencastify.com/

Screencast-O-Matic: https://screencast-o-matic.com/

Technology Tools for "Get to Know Me" Activities

Adobe Spark: https://spark.adobe.com/

Book Creator (app): https://bookcreator.com/

Google Sites: https://sites.google.com/

Google Slides: https://www.google.com/slides/about/

Microsoft PowerPoint: https://www.microsoft.com/

ShowMe (app): http://www.showme.com/

Weebly: https://www.weebly.com/

Wix: https://www.wix.com/

Translation Programs and Devices

ili: https://iamili.com/

Pilot: https://www.waverlylabs.com/

(For further resources, see Table 3.6.)

Universal Design for Learning (UDL) Resources

Center for Applied Special Technology: http://www.cast.org/

National Center on Universal Design for Learning: http://www.udlcenter.org/

Videoconferencing/Video Recording Tools

VoiceThread: https://voicethread.com/

Zoom: https://zoom.us/

Websites That Discuss the Historical Contributions of Marginalized Groups

See Tables 3.7 and 3.8.

REFERENCES

Adkins, T. A. 2012. "Can't nobody sleep" and other characteristics of culturally responsive English instruction. *Multicultural Perspectives*, *14*(2), 73–81.

Al-Attar, G., De Meyer, S., El-Gibaly, O., Michielsen, K., Animosa, L. H., and Mmari, K. 2017. "A boy would be friends with boys and a girl with girls": Gender norms in early adolescent friendships in Egypt and Belgium. *Journal of Adolescent Health*, *61*, 30–34.

Allen, R. and Steed, E. A. 2016. Culturally responsive pyramid model practices: Program-wide positive behavior support for young children. *Topics in Early Childhood Special Education*, *36*(3), 165–175.

Armstrong, T. 2009. *Multiple intelligences in the classroom* (3rd ed.). Alexandria, VA: Association for Supervision and Curriculum Development.

Basu, S., Zuo, X., Lou, C., Acharya, R., and Lundgren, R. 2017. Learning to be gendered: Gender socialization in early adolescence among urban poor in Delhi, India, and Shanghai, China. *Journal of Adolescent Health*, *61*, 24–29.

Blum, R. W., Mmari, K., and Moreau, C. 2017. It begins at 10: How gender expectations shape early adolescence around the world. *Journal of Adolescent Health*, *61*, 3–4.

Brown, A. and Patton, E. 2017. The narrowing, but persistent, gender gap in pay. Pew Research Center [online]. Available at: http://www.pewresearch.org/fact-tank/2017/04/03/gender-pay-gap-facts/. Accessed on October 10, 2017.

Brummelman, E., Thomaes, S., Overbeek, G., Orobio de Castro, B., Van den Hout, M., Bushman, B., and Gauthier, I. 2014. On feeding those hungry for praise: Person praise backfires in children with low self-esteem. *Journal of Experimental Psychology: General*, *143*(1), 9–14.

Bullock, H. E., Wyche, K. F., and Williams, W. R. 2001. Media images of the poor. *Journal of Social Issues*, *57*(2), 229–246.

Bussey, K. and Bandura, A. 1999. Social cognitive theory of gender development and differentiation. *Psychological Review*, *106*(4), 676–713.

Carroll, A. and Mendos, L. R. 2017. *State-sponsored homophobia: A world survey of sexual orientation laws: Criminalisation, protection and recognition.* Geneva: International Lesbian, Gay, Bisexual, Trans and Intersex Association. Available at: http://ilga.org/downloads/2017/ILGA_State_Sponsored_Homophobia_2017_WEB.pdf. Accessed on October 15, 2017.

Chase, E. and Walker, R. 2013. The co-construction of shame in the context of poverty: Beyond a threat to the social bond. *Sociology*, *47*(4), 739–754.

The Chocolate Project. 2017. [Online]. Available at: http://www.real-projects.org/the-centre-for -extraordinary-work/the-chocolate-project/. Accessed on October 13, 2017.

Clarke, E., DeNora, T., and Vuoskoski, J. 2015. Music, empathy and cultural understanding. *Physics of Life Reviews*, *15*, 61–88.

Coffey, G. 2012. Literacy and technology: Integrating technology with small group, peer-led discussions of literature. *International Electronic Journal of Elementary Education*, *4*(2), 395–405.

Collins, R. L. 2011. Content analysis of gender roles in media: Where are we now and where should we go? *Sex Roles*, *64*(3), 290–298.

Comer, D. and Lenaghan, J. 2013. Enhancing discussions in the asynchronous online classroom: The lack of face-to-face interaction does not lessen the lesson. *Journal of Management Education*, *37*(2), 261–294.

Curtis, D. 2001. Project-based learning: Real-world issues motivate students [online]. Available at: https:// www.edutopia.org/project-based-learning-student-motivation. Accessed on October 13, 2017.

Daniel, J. R., Santos, A. J., Peceguina, I., and Vaughn, B. E. 2015. Affiliative structures and social competence in Portuguese preschool children. *Developmental Psychology*, *51*(7), 905–912.

Dorfman, S. and Rosenberg, R. 2013. Building a community that includes all learners. *Social Studies and the Young Learner*, *25*(3), 5–8.

Douglas, O., Burton, K., and Reese-Durham, N. 2008. The effects of the multiple intelligence teaching strategy on the academic achievement of eighth grade math students. *Journal of Instructional Psychology*, *35*(2), 182–187.

Dweck, C. S. 2007. The perils and promises of praise. *Educational Leadership*, *65*(2), 34–39.

Eksi, G. 2009. Multiple short story activities for very young learners with multiple tastes. *Ekev Academic Review*, *13*(40), 51–68.

Eliot, L. 2009. *Pink brain, blue brain: How small differences grow into troublesome gaps—and what we can do about it.* Boston, MA: Houghton Mifflin Harcourt.

Elliot-Engel, J. and Westfall-Rudd, D. 2016. What is a culturally-responsive educator? *Agricultural Education Magazine*, *89*(2), 13–14.

Evans, J. and Williams, R. 2015. Stuttering in film media—Investigation of a stereotype. *Procedia— Social and Behavioral Sciences*, *193*, 337.

Figueiredo, A. R. and Abreu, T. 2015. Suicide among LGBT individuals. *European Psychiatry*, *30*, 1815.

Fine, C. 2010. *Delusions of gender: How our minds, society, and neurosexism create difference* (1st ed.). New York, NY: W. W. Norton.

Fung, W. K. and Cheng, R. W. Y. 2017. Effect of school pretend play on preschoolers' social competence in peer interactions: Gender as a potential moderator. *Early Childhood Education Journal*, *45*(1), 35–42.

Gardner, H. 1983. *Frames of mind: The theory of multiple intelligences.* New York, NY: Basic Books.

Gardner, H. 1999. *Intelligence reframed: Multiple intelligences for the 21st century.* New York, NY: Basic Books.

Gardner, H. 2006. *Multiple intelligences: New horizons.* New York, NY: Basic Books.

Gardner, H. 2011a. *Frames of mind: The theory of multiple intelligences* (3rd ed.). New York, NY: Basic Books.

Gardner, H. 2011b. Promoting learner engagement using multiple intelligences and choice-based instruction. *Adult Basic Education & Literacy Journal*, 5(2), 97–101.

Gay, G. 2010. *Culturally responsive teaching: Theory, research, and practice*. New York, NY: Teachers College Press.

Gay, G. 2013. Cultural diversity and multicultural education. *Curriculum Inquiry*, 43(1), 48–70.

GLSEN. 2017. "No promo homo" laws. Gay, Lesbian & Straight Education Network [online]. Available at: https://www.glsen.org/learn/policy/issues/nopromohomo. Accessed on October 10, 2017.

Golden, J. C. and Jacoby, J. W. 2017. Playing princess: Preschool girls' interpretations of gender stereotypes in Disney Princess media. *Sex Roles*, 79(5–6), 1–15.

Hamilton, K., Piacentini, M., Banister, E., Barrios, A., Blocker, C., Coleman, C., Ekici, A., Gorge, H., Hutton, M., Passerard, F., and Saatcioglu, B. 2014. Poverty in consumer culture: Towards a transformative social representation. *Journal of Marketing Management*, 30(17–18), 1–25.

Han, H. and Thomas, M. 2010. No child misunderstood: Enhancing early childhood teachers' multicultural responsiveness to the social competence of diverse children. *Early Childhood Education Journal*, 37(6), 469–476.

Hasler, B., Spanlang, B., and Slater, M. 2017. Virtual race transformation reverses racial in-group bias. *PLoS One*, 12(4), e0174965.

Hegewisch, A., Phil, M., and Williams-Baron, E. 2017. The gender wage gap: 2016; Earnings differences by gender, race, and ethnicity. Institute for Women's Policy [online]. Available at: https://iwpr.org/publications/gender-wage-gap-2016-earnings-differences-gender-race-ethnicity/. Accessed on October 10, 2017.

Hernández-Torrano, D., Ferrándiz, C., Ferrando, M., Prieto, L., and Del Carmen Fernández, M. 2014. The theory of multiple intelligences in the identification of high-ability students. *Anales De Psicología/Annals of Psychology*, 30(1), 192–200.

Hill, C., Corbett, C., and Rose, A. 2010. *Why so few? Women in science, technology, engineering, and mathematics*. Washington, DC: AAUW. Available at: http://www.aauw.org/files/2013/02/Why-So-Few-Women-in-Science-Technology-Engineering-and-Mathematics.pdf. Accessed on October 10, 2017.

Ivers, K. S. and Barron, A. E. 2014. *Digital content creation in schools*. Santa Barbara, CA: ABC-CLIO.

Johnson, D. W. and Johnson, R. T. 2014. Cooperative learning in 21st century. *Anales De PsicologíA/ Annals of Psychology*, 30(3), 841–851.

Johnson-Harris, K. and Mundschenk, N. 2014. Working effectively with students with BD in a general education classroom: The case for universal design for learning. *Clearing House: A Journal of Educational Strategies, Issues and Ideas*, 87(4), 168–174.

Joseph, N. M., Viesca, K. M., and Bianco, M. 2016. Black female adolescents and racism in schools: Experiences in a colorblind society. *High School Journal*, 100(1), 4–25.

Kaeppler, A. K. and Erath, S. A. 2017. Linking social anxiety with social competence in early adolescence: Physiological and coping moderators. *Journal of Abnormal Child Psychology*, 45(2), 371–384.

Kamins, M. L. and Dweck, C. S. 1999. Person versus process praise and criticism: Implications for contingent self-worth and coping. *Developmental Psychology*, 35(3), 835–847.

Kelso, T. 2015. Still trapped in the U.S. media's closet: Representations of gender-variant, pre-adolescent children. *Journal of Homosexuality*, 62(8), 1–40.

Kirsch, A. C. and Murnen, S. K. 2015. "Hot" girls and "cool dudes": Examining the prevalence of the heterosexual script in American children's television media. *Psychology of Popular Media Culture, 4*(1), 18–30.

Koutamanis, M., Vossen, H. G. M., Peter, J., and Valkenburg, P. M. 2013. Practice makes perfect: The longitudinal effect of adolescents' instant messaging on their ability to initiate offline friendships. *Computers in Human Behavior, 29*(6), 2265–2272.

Kukovec, M. 2014. Cross-curricular teaching: The case of Mark Haddon's the curious incident of the dog in the night-time. *ELOPE: English Language Overseas Perspectives and Enquiries, 11*(1), 137–150.

La Macchia, S. T., Louis, W. R., Hornsey, M. J., Thai, M., and Barlow, F. K. 2016. The whitewashing effect: Using racial contact to signal trustworthiness and competence. *Personality and Social Psychology Bulletin, 42*(1), 118–129.

La Porte, A. 2016. Efficacy of the arts in a transdisciplinary learning experience for culturally diverse fourth graders. *International Electronic Journal of Elementary Education, 8*(3), 467–480.

Ladson-Billings, G. 2009. *The dreamkeepers: Successful teachers of African American children* (2nd ed.). San Francisco, CA: Jossey-Bass.

Lambeth, D. T. and Smith, A. M. 2016. Pre-service teachers' perceptions of culturally responsive teacher preparation. *Journal of Negro Education, 85*(1), 46–58.

Link, B. G. and Phelan, J. C. 2014. Mental illness stigma and the sociology of mental health. In R. J. Johnson, R. J., Turner, and B. G. Link (Eds.), *Sociology of mental health* (pp. 75–100). New York, NY: Springer International Publishing.

Lynch, M. 2014. 6 ways teachers can foster cultural awareness in the classroom. Education Week [online]. Available at: http://blogs.edweek.org/edweek/education_futures/2014/11/6_ways_teachers_can _foster_cultural_awareness_in_the_classroom.html. Accessed on October 14, 2017.

Maister, L., Slater, M., Sanchez-Vives, M. V., and Tsakiris, M. 2015. Changing bodies changes minds: Owning another body affects social cognition. *Trends in Cognitive Sciences, 19*(1), 6–12.

Makarova, E. and Herzog, W. 2015. Trapped in the gender stereotype? The image of science among secondary school students and teachers. *Equality, Diversity and Inclusion: An International Journal, 34*(2), 106–123.

Martin, R. 2017. Gender and emotion stereotypes in children's television. *Journal of Broadcasting & Electronic Media, 61*(3), 499–517.

Martins, N. and Harrison, K. 2012. Racial and gender differences in the relationship between children's television use and self-esteem. *Communication Research, 39*(3), 338–357.

Mclaughlin, B. and Rodriguez, N. S. 2017. Identifying with a stereotype: The divergent effects of exposure to homosexual television characters. *Journal of Homosexuality, 64*(9), 1196–1213.

Mohr, R. and Purdie-Vaughns, V. 2015. Diversity within women of color: Why experiences change felt stigma. *Sex Roles, 73*(9–10), 391–398.

National Center on Universal Design for Learning. 2014. What is UDL? [online]. Available at: http://www.udlcenter.org/aboutudl/whatisudl. Accessed on October 16, 2017.

Nölke, A. 2018. Making diversity conform? An intersectional, longitudinal analysis of LGBT-specific mainstream media advertisements. *Journal of Homosexuality, 65*(2), 224–255.

OECD. 2015. *Students, Computers and Learning: Making the Connection.* PISA, OECD Publishing. http://dx.doi.org/10.1787/9789264239555-en

Page, M. 2017. Forgotten youth: Homeless LGBT youth of color and the runaway and homeless youth act. *Northwestern Journal of Law & Social Policy*, *12*(2), 17–45.

Parrott, S. and Parrott, C. 2015a. Law & disorder: The portrayal of mental illness in U.S. crime dramas. *Journal of Broadcasting & Electronic Media*, *59*(4), 640–657.

Parrott, S. and Parrott, C. 2015b. U.S. television's "Mean World" for white women: The portrayal of gender and race on fictional crime dramas. *Sex Roles*, *73*(1), 70–82.

Partnership for 21st Century Learning. 2007. *Framework for 21st Century Learning* [online]. Available at: http://www.p21.org/our-work/p21-framework. Accessed on September 18, 2017.

Perez, L. and Beltran, J. 2008. A Spanish intervention programme for students with special education needs: Effects on intellectual capacity and academic achievement. *European Journal of Special Needs Education*, *23*(2), 147–156.

Permenter, L. 2012. Preventing discrimination in services for homeless LGBT youth [online]. Available at: http://escholarship.org/uc/item/5sp9v446. Accessed on October 15, 2017.

Pietri, E. S., Johnson, I. R., and Ozgumus, E. 2017. One size may not fit all: Exploring how the intersection of race and gender and stigma consciousness predict effective identity-safe cues for black women. *Journal of Experimental Social Psychology*, *78*, 291–306.

Popa, D. and Gavriliu, D. 2015. Gender representations and digital media. *Procedia—Social and Behavioral Sciences*, *180*, 1199–1206.

Rao, K. and Torres, C. 2017. Supporting academic and affective learning processes for English language learners with universal design for learning. *TESOL Quarterly*, *51*(2), 460–472.

Ridgeway, C. L. 2009. Framed before we know it: How gender shapes social relations. *Gender & Society*, *23*(2), 145–160.

Robinson, M. D., Fetterman, A. K., Hopkins, K., and Krishnakumar, S. 2013. Losing one's cool. *Personality and Social Psychology Bulletin*, *39*(10), 1268–1279.

Rychly, L. and Graves, E. 2012. Teacher characteristics for culturally responsive pedagogy. *Multicultural Perspectives*, *14*(1), 44–49.

Samples, B. 1992. Using learning modalities to celebrate intelligence. *Educational Leadership*, *50*(2), 62–66.

Segal, C. 2017. Eight states censor LGBTQ topics in school. Now, a lawsuit is challenging that. PBS Newshour [online]. Available at: http://www.pbs.org/newshour/updates/lgbtq-issues-class-lawsuit-utah/. Accessed on October 10, 2017.

Shrum, L., Wyer, R., Jr., and O'Guinn, T. 1998. The effects of television consumption on social perceptions: The use of priming procedures to investigate psychological processes. *Journal of Consumer Research*, *24*(4), 447–458.

Simpson, C. C., Kwitowski, M., Boutte, R., Gow, R. W., and Mazzeo, S. E. 2016. Messages about appearance, food, weight and exercise in "tween" television. *Eating Behaviors*, *23*, 70–75.

Skipper, Y. and Douglas, K. 2012. Is no praise good praise? Effects of positive feedback on children's and university students' responses to subsequent failures. *British Journal of Educational Psychology*, *82*(2), 327–339.

Smith, S. L., Choueiti, M., and Pieper, K. 2016. *Inequality in 800 popular films: Examining portrayals of gender, race/ethnicity, LGBT, and disability from 2007–2015*. Annenberg Foundation [online]. Available at: http://annenberg.usc.edu/sites/default/files/2017/04/10/MDSCI_Inequality_in_800_Films_FINAL.pdf. Accessed on November 10, 2017.

Social Competence. 2016. In J. L. Longe (Ed.), *The Gale encyclopedia of psychology* (3rd ed., Vol. 2, pp. 1105–1112). Farmington Hills, MI: Gale.

Sternberg, R. J. 1994. Diversifying instruction and assessment. *Educational Forum*, *59*(1), 47–52.

Strauss, V. 2017. The surprising thing Google learned about its employees—and what it means for today's students [online]. Available at: https://www.washingtonpost.com/news/answer-sheet/wp/2017/12/20/the-surprising-thing-google-learned-about-its-employees-and-what-it-means-for-todays-students/?utm_term=.02cb5f0e0413. Accessed on January 13, 2018.

Su, D., Irwin, J. A., Fisher, C., Ramos, A., Kelley, M., Mendoza, D. A. R., and Coleman, J. D. 2016. Mental health disparities within the LGBT population: A Comparison between transgender and nontransgender individuals. *Transgender Health*, *1*(1), 12–20.

Sun, C., Liberman, R., Butler, A., Lee, S., and Webb, R. 2015. Shifting receptions: Asian American stereotypes and the exploration of comprehensive media literacy. *Communication Review*, *18*(4), 294–314.

Tran, A., Lee, R., and Zárate, M. 2011. Cultural socialization as a moderator of friendships and social competence. *Cultural Diversity and Ethnic Minority Psychology*, *17*(4), 456–461.

Trash to Treasure. n.d. [online]. Available at: http://wveis.k12.wv.us/teach21/public/project/Guide.cfm?upid=3512&tsele1=1&tsele2=102. Accessed on October 13, 2017.

Tukachinsky, R. 2015. Where we have been and where we can go from here: Looking to the future in research on media, race, and ethnicity. *Journal of Social Issues*, *71*(1), 186–199.

Tukachinsky, R., Mastro, R., and Yarchi, M. 2017. The effect of prime time television ethnic/racial stereotypes on Latino and black Americans: A longitudinal national level study. *Journal of Broadcasting & Electronic Media*, *61*(3), 538–556.

Ullucci, K. and Howard, T. 2015. Pathologizing the poor: Implications for preparing teachers to work in high-poverty schools. *Urban Education*, *50*(2), 170–193.

Vermonden, C. and Alcock, P. 2013 (Winter). Using multiple intelligences to promote nature education. *Green Teacher*, 12–15.

Vossen, H. G. M. and Valkenburg, P. M. 2016. Do social media foster or curtail adolescents' empathy? A longitudinal study. *Computers in Human Behavior*, *63*, 118–124.

Walker, R., Kyomuhendo, G., Chase, E., Choudhry, S., Gubrium, E., Nicola, J., Lødemel, I., Mathew, L., Mwiine, A., Pellissery, S., and Ming, Y. 2013. Poverty in global perspective: Is shame a common denominator? *Journal of Social Policy*, *42*, 215–233.

Wall, C. 2017. Bridging understanding between preservice teachers and diverse students through service-learning. *Teaching Education*, *28*(2), 178–193.

Ward, L. M. and Aubrey, J. S. 2017. *Watching gender: How stereotypes in movies and on TV impact kids' development*. San Francisco, CA: Common Sense.

Weinstein, C., Tomlinson-Clarke, S., and Curran, M. 2004. Toward a conception of culturally responsive classroom management.*Journal of Teacher Education*, *55*(1), 25–38.

Williams, M. and Korn, J. 2017. Othering and fear. *Journal of Communication Inquiry*, *41*(1), 22–41.

Wohl, A. 2017. Reflections of disability in the mirror of culture. *Human Rights*, *42*(4), 22–23.

Yu, C., Zuo, X., Blum, R. W., Tolman, D. L., Kågesten, A., Mmari, K, De Meyer, S., Michielsen, K., Basu, S., Acharya, R., Lian, Q., and Chaohua, L. 2017. Marching to a different drummer: A cross-cultural comparison of young adolescents who challenge gender norms. *Journal of Adolescent Health*, *61*, 48–54.

Ch3. Resource Page: All About Me

Using a technology tool of your choice, create an *All About Me* digital story.

- Brainstorm facts you want to share about yourself, including your cultural background, what has been the most impactful experience in your life, and three other things and why you chose these (e.g., family, hobby, career goals, favorite dish, movie, book, music, holiday, and sport).

- Research and learn more about the chosen facts. Provide background information about each of your facts.

- Outline and write a script for your story.

- Design and sequence the storyboards for the project.

- Gather and create the multimedia elements needed for the project.

- Develop the project.

- Share your final project. Limit your presentation to 10 minutes.

- Compare and contrast your story with others, looking at similarities and what makes them unique.

Ch3. Resource Page: GEG

Write what you know about how greetings, emotions, and gestures differ across cultures.

Watch the following YouTube videos or find other Internet resources to learn more about how greetings, emotions, and gestures differ across cultures.

- https://youtu.be/QLISC-opIOY
- https://youtu.be/JChxT9Yv2iw
- https://youtu.be/YKyRbyRhMnw

Write what you learned about how greetings, emotions, and gestures differ across cultures, including anything that may have surprised you.

Ch3. Resource Page: Media Project 1

Create a team with two or three additional students, and select one of the following groups. Each team should have a different group.

- People with disabilities

- LGBTQ+ individuals

- Females

- Non-White males

- Low socioeconomic-status individuals

Work with your team to identify, provide examples of, and discuss how the media both positively and negatively represents your selected group. Media may include pictures in catalogs (school or retail related), video clips (e.g., commercials, television programs, and movies), books (picture books, textbooks, etc.), brochures, and so on. Create a presentation (10 to 15 minutes) using a presentation app or software of your choice and be ready to share it with other teams. The following are the criteria:

- Project clearly reflects the select group and the impact media has on the group (includes positive and negative examples).

- Connections are made to the readings and other research.

- A variety of media is represented.

- Presentation includes a conclusion, recommendations, and activities of how educators can ensure their group is equitably represented in the classroom and across the curriculum.

Ch3. Resource Page: Media Project 2

Sit with three or four other people and watch the video at https://youtu.be/-uJAxNuyiF8.

It is a parody of a "Mr. Clean" commercial with role reversal. The male is the homemaker, females are making the mess, and "Mr. Clean" is a Black woman.

Discuss the video and reflect on the counter-stereotypic roles portrayed by the actors and how this affects the effectiveness of the advertisement.

Working in your group, find an advertisement on YouTube that perpetuates stereotypes. Recreate the ad using role reversals and inclusion to eliminate the stereotypes associated with the ad.

In addition, find an ad that does not perpetuate stereotypes (dad stays at home while the mother works, two moms are raising a family, etc.). If possible, choose an ad based on the same type of product (e.g., laundry detergent).

Present your work, showing and discussing the original ad first, followed by your ad and comparative analysis, and an ad that does not perpetuate stereotypes. Conclude with your reflection and assessment of the ads and why you think advertisers portray social groups the way they do and how this may impact students' social perceptions.

Ch3. Resource Page: Born Poor

Work with one or two people to create a digital story about a person who was born poor and became known for their notable achievements and contributions. Examples include Oprah Winfrey, Abraham Lincoln, Dr. B. R. Ambedkar, J. K. Rowling, and Leonardo Del Vecchio. You are not limited to these examples, nor does the person need to be famous to be considered successful. Each group should choose a different person. Use the Internet and other sources to learn more about your selected person. Use a technology tool of your choice.

Follow the following steps:

1. Decide on a person.

2. Research and learn more about the person and his or her accomplishments.

3. Write the script for the story.

4. Design and sequence the storyboards for the project.

5. Gather and create the multimedia elements needed for the project (e.g., audio, video, and graphics).

6. Develop the project.

7. Share projects and discuss what you learned, including how learning about these individuals impacted your perception of impoverished students.

8. Limit your presentation to 10 minutes.

Chapter 4

Global Competence

OVERVIEW

The Association of American Colleges & Universities (AAC&U), Partnership for 21st Century Learning (P21), and the International Society for Technology in Education (ISTE) stress the importance of preparing students for our digitally and globally interconnected world. The AAC&U notes the importance of global learning and intercultural studies; the P21 emphasizes the significance of global awareness and learning to collaborate with others representing diverse cultures, religions, and lifestyles; and ISTE advocates teaching students to be global collaborators, using technology to help students broaden their perspectives by connecting with learners from different backgrounds and cultures (ISTE 2016; Kuh 2008; Partnership for 21st Century Learning 2007). Johnson and Johnson (2014) discuss global interdependence and the importance of students having the necessary skills to work cooperatively with others different from themselves. This chapter provides an overview of global competence, investigating the importance of working together, supporting global competence, what the world teaches us, and how technology can support global competence.

GLOBAL COMPETENCE

There are many skills associated with global competence. These include the ability to appreciate different cultures and understand that behaviors, beliefs, and values are frequently connected to a person's culture; the capacity to successfully communicate and exchange ideas with people from different backgrounds; the proficiency to effectively evaluate information to discriminate against fact and opinion; the desire to seek deeper understanding and recognize bias; the empathy, openness, and respect to consider multiple perspectives; the humility to recognize that knowledge is not finite and grows and evolves as we learn more about the world; the aptitude to engage in divergent thinking; and the ability to use technology to learn about and engage in our increasing, interconnected world (Young 2016). Morris (2017) stresses the importance of building students' global awareness and competence at a young age.

Educators can begin building young students' awareness of different cultures through picture books. A compilation of picture books featuring stories from around the world are available at What Do We Do All Day (https://www.whatdowedoallday.com/around-world-childrens-books/). This site provides a book list for teaching children about social justice and other global competency topics, too. Additional resources are available at Kid World Citizen (see https://kidworldcitizen.org/category/literature/). Mladic-Morales (2014, para 1) notes, "Children's books with multicultural settings and characters can transport us on a global adventure, dispelling negative stereotypes, teaching tolerance and respect, encouraging pride in kids' cultural heritage, and showcasing universal human emotions and feelings." Children can compare and discuss folktales and fairy tales from around the world, including cultural variations of *Cinderella* (see https://kidworldcitizen.org/cinderella-story-around-the-world/) or *Little Red Riding Hood* (see https://kidworldcitizen.org/little-red-riding-hood-3-multicultural-versions/), also, providing students with insight about different cultural traditions and values.

Duncan (2017) suggests several ideas for engaging students in their travels around the world, including creating and discussing the purpose of passports, mapping their travels on a world map, comparing weather conditions along the way, incorporating cultural arts and crafts representative of each travel location, taking virtual field trips or discussing pictures and articles relative to the destination, cooking and eating authentic food from the country, connecting with pen pals, learning about and charting holidays and other events celebrated in the country, becoming knowledgeable about different cultures' etiquette, and learning about each country's official language, including some basic phrases and words, spoken and written. Students' passports serve as a record of their journey. A small box or *suitcase*, decorated as they travel, can store students' work, artifacts, and souvenirs. Older students can increase their global awareness and competence through age-appropriate books, also, discussing inequity, discrimination, poverty, and other global issues. In addition to books, teachers can help build students' global competence by using technology to provide authentic, real-world, cultural learning experiences.

As educators prepare their students for the challenges, demands, and opportunities of an interdependent, global society, it is essential to reflect upon how nations are currently working together, how educators can help students develop global competence, what the world continues to teach us, and how the Internet and advancements in technology can contribute to students' global competence.

Working Together

Having experienced the horror and destruction caused by two world wars, nations got together and formed the United Nations. The Charter of the United Nations was signed on June 26, 1945, and came into force on October 24, 1945, with the purposes of maintaining international peace and security, developing friendly relations among nations, achieving international cooperation in solving international problems, and serving as the forum for helping nations achieve these common goals (United Nations n.d.). Since its creation, the members of the United Nations have worked together to address issues confronting humanity, including human rights, gender equality, sustainability, climate change, terrorism, peace, and more (United Nations n.d.). The United Nations' 2030 Agenda for Sustainable Development addresses these issues, with the goals of ending poverty and hunger; protecting the planet; ensuring everyone can enjoy prosperous and fulfilling lives; fostering just, inclusive, and peaceful societies; and strengthening global partnerships by 2030 (United Nations 2015). There are 17 sustainable development goals (see Table 4.1). Addition information, including progress for each goal, is available at https://sustainabledevelopment.un.org/.

Shortly after its formation, the United Nations created the UN Educational, Scientific and Cultural Organization (UNESCO). UNESCO is responsible for coordinating international cooperation in education, science, culture, and communication (UNESCO n.d.). In its efforts to support 21st-century education, UNESCO is leading the Global Education 2030 Agenda through Sustainable Development Goal 4: Ensure inclusive and equitable quality education and promote lifelong learning opportunities for all. This goal includes universal, free, and high-quality preprimary, primary, and secondary education for all girls and boys; equal access for men and women to quality technical/vocational and higher education; gender equality and inclusive education; and universal literacy and numeracy (Education 2030 Framework for Action 2015).

Table 4.1. UN Sustainable Development Goals

Short Name	Goal
No Poverty	End poverty in all its forms everywhere.
Zero Hunger	End hunger, achieve food security and improved nutrition and promote sustainable agriculture.
Good Health and Well-Being	Ensure healthy lives and promote well-being for all at all ages.
Quality Education	Ensure inclusive and equitable quality education and promote lifelong learning opportunities for all.
Gender Equality	Achieve gender equality and empower all women and girls.
Clean Water and Sanitation	Ensure availability and sustainable management of water and sanitation for all.
Affordable and Clean Energy	Ensure access to affordable, reliable, sustainable and modern energy for all.
Decent Work and Economic Growth	Promote sustained, inclusive and sustainable economic growth, full and productive employment and decent work for all.
Industry, Innovation, and Infrastructure	Build resilient infrastructure, promote inclusive and sustainable industrialization and foster innovation.
Reduced Inequalities	Reduce inequality within and among countries.
Sustainable Cities and Communities	Make cities and human settlements inclusive, safe, resilient and sustainable.
Responsible Consumption and Production	Ensure sustainable consumption and production patterns.
Climate Action	Take urgent action to combat climate change and its impacts.
Life Below Water	Conserve and sustainably use the oceans, seas and marine resources for sustainable development.
Life on Land	Protect, restore and promote sustainable use of terrestrial ecosystems, sustainably manage forests, combat desertification, and halt and reverse land degradation and halt biodiversity loss.
Peace, Justice, and Strong Institutions	Promote peaceful and inclusive societies for sustainable development, provide access to justice for all and build effective, accountable and inclusive institutions at all levels.
Partnerships for the Goals	Strengthen the means of implementation and revitalize the global partnership for sustainable development.

Source: United Nations. Retrieved from https://sustainabledevelopment.un.org/. © United Nations. Reprinted with the permission of the United Nations.

In addition to the United Nations, the importance of global learning and outreach is evident throughout many educational, government, and business institutions. The P21 emphasizes the significance of students using 21st-century skills (e.g., creativity and innovation, critical thinking and problem solving, communication, and collaboration) to learn about and work with others from diverse cultures, religions, and lifestyles from other nations (Partnership for 21st Century Learning 2007). Think Global, a UK organization, stresses critical and creative thinking, self-awareness and open-mindedness toward difference, understanding of global issues and power relationships, and optimism and action for a better world as part of global learning (Think Global n.d.). Think Global identifies eight overlapping components of global learning: global citizenship, interdependence, social justice, conflict resolution, diversity, values and perceptions, human rights, and sustainable development. The Center for Global Education at Asia Society works with educators, businesses, and government officials to change policies and practice to support global education. The Center is currently focusing on how to educate all students for employability and citizenship in a global era, targeting the UN Sustainable Development Goal 4 (Asia Society 2017b). While many countries are making progress toward a more cooperative, interconnected, and equitable world, there remain those who continue to focus on a more nationalistic, elite, and competitive orientation (Hammond 2016).

Supporting Global Competence

Global learning leads to global competence. The Council of Chief State School Officers (CCSSO)/Asia Society task force defines global competence as "the capacity and disposition to understand and act on issues of global significance" (Mansilla and Jackson 2011, xiii). In order to become globally competent, students need opportunities to investigate matters of global significance, recognize their own and others' perspectives and communicate their positions clearly, and learn how to develop and carry out informed action plans (Mansilla and Jackson 2011). The Asia Society notes (Asia Society 2017a, para 4):

> Global competence is not restricted to knowing about other cultures and other perspectives. In addition to knowledge of the world, a globally competent citizen exhibits habits like critical thinking, rational optimism, innovation, empathy, and awareness of the influences of culture on individual behavior and world events.

In our globally and digitally interconnected world, students' success will depend on their global competence. Students need to engage in high-order thinking skills, communicate carefully and respectfully with diverse audiences, work cooperatively, and approach problems from multiple perspectives (Mansilla and Jackson 2011).

Frameworks, outcomes, and rubrics are available to assist educators as they implement global learning in their schools and classrooms. The P21 published the *Framework for State Action on Global Education* to provide states with strategies for implementing global learning into classroom instruction. In order to successfully participate in a global, interconnect world, P21 believes students need to:

- explore their own cultures, make comparisons with other cultures, and investigate global issues and challenges;

- improve their critical-thinking, problem-solving, perspective-taking, and research skills; and

- develop awareness of cultural diversity and global issues (Partnership for 21st Century Learning 2014, 1–2).

Teachers need to:

- create and sustain creative learning environments;

- continually develop understanding of and applications for inquiry-based pedagogical approaches;

- integrate global content into classroom instruction; and

- utilize next-generation technologies in curricular practices (Partnership for 21st Century Learning 2014, 2).

The *Framework for State Action on Global Education* (Partnership for 21st Century Learning 2014) offers the six essential elements for implementing global learning in schools (see Table 4.2).

P21 provides K–12 global competence grade-level indicators, too (Partnership for 21st Century Learning n.d.). For example, in kindergarten and first grade, students demonstrate a global perspective through multiple learning opportunities to compare other cultures to their own. Each indicator is broken down into four main areas: Understanding, Investigating, Connecting, and Integrating. For Understanding, K–1 students articulate the role of culture in everyday life by describing one's own cultural traditions and comparing and contrasting with classmates' and global peers' cultural traditions. For Investigating, K–1 students ask questions, use multiple resources, and learn about global peers. For Connecting, K–1 students demonstrate the ability to work with a peer, and with collaborative peer groups, in face-to-face and online mediums. For Integrating, K–1 students demonstrate the ability to use knowledge of their own culture and other cultures to describe, explain, analyze, or create. For example, a student who celebrates Christmas may explain why he/she celebrates Christmas and why other people celebrate Hanukkah. P21's K–12 global competence grade-level indicators guide is available at http://www.p21.org/storage/documents/Global_Education/P21_K-12_Global_Ed_Indicators.pdf.

The Asia Society provides performance outcomes and rubrics for global competencies in leadership, mathematics, the sciences, the arts, history and social studies, and English language arts. A definition, performance outcomes, rubrics, and "I can" statements are provided for each topic. Each topic addresses the four competencies that define a globally competent student (Mansilla and Jackson 2011, 11):

- Investigate the world beyond their immediate environment, framing significant problems and conducting a well-crafted and age-appropriate research.

- Recognize perspectives, others' and their own, articulating and explaining such perspectives thoughtfully and respectfully.

- Communicate ideas effectively with diverse audiences, bridging geographic, linguistic, ideological, and cultural barriers.

- Take action to improve conditions, viewing themselves as players in the world and participating reflectively.

For example, students demonstrate global competencies in leadership by *investigating the world* (e.g., framing questions, analyzing and synthesizing relevant evidence, and drawing reasonable conclusions about global issues), *recognizing perspectives* (e.g., recognize, articulate, and apply an understanding of different perspectives, including his/her own), *communicating ideas* (e.g., select and apply appropriate tools and strategies to communicate and collaborate effectively, meeting the needs and expectations of diverse individuals and groups), and *taking action* (e.g., translate his/her ideas, concerns, and findings into appropriate and responsible individual or

Table 4.2. Essential Elements and Strategies for Implementing Global Learning

Essential Element	Strategies
1. Adopt Global Competency Standards for Students and Teachers	Define student and teacher global competency to guide state and district global education agendas.
2. Effective and Scalable Teacher Support, Resources, and Tools	Provide teachers with resources and tools for integrating global themes and problem-based learning that focuses on global issues throughout the curriculum.
	Implement a recognition system to support and inspire professional development on global issues.
	Require preservice teachers to demonstrate global competence and the ability to integrate global content throughout the curriculum.
3. A New Approach to Language Instruction	Mandate a statewide dual language/immersion program that begins in elementary school and continues through high school.
	Redesign high school world language courses to include a greater emphasis on the study of global and international affairs; on the economies, societies, and cultures of other nations; and on survival language skills.
4. Whole-School Models	Create new schools that focus on international education.
	Solicit businesses, foundations, and nonprofit groups to support and assist with the implementation of new school models.
5. Networking and Recognizing Districts, Schools, and Educators	Establish networks to strengthen the dissemination of tools and resources and knowledge for supporting global content, teacher support, language instruction, and new school models.
	Create recognition programs for students, teachers, principals, schools, and districts to inspire educators and administrators to adopt innovative global education practices.
	Use partnerships outside of government to drive the global education agenda.
	Connect state departments of education with businesses (and other relevant agencies) to develop county or community profiles of international assets, including local businesses, languages spoken, and countries represented.
6. Global Experiences for Students and Educators	Create policies that provide support for and commitment to global experiences for educators, students, and administrators, including exchange programs, virtual global experiences, and global academic collaborations and competitions.

collaborative actions to improve conditions). Students demonstrate global competencies in different subject areas by investigating the world, recognizing perspectives, communicating ideas, and taking action too. For example, in the arts, students work in and through the arts to investigate the world, recognize his/her own and others' perspectives in and through the art, communicate his/her ideas and feelings in and through the arts to diverse audiences, and translate ideas and findings into artistic expressions intended to increase awareness and improve conditions. In mathematics, students use mathematics to model and investigate a given issue, situation, or event; recognize the impact of his/her mathematical analyses on himself/herself and others; communicate and defend his/her mathematical thinking, approaches, representations, solution, and decisions; and advocate for, engage in, and reflect on plausible and responsible actions that are supported by his/her mathematics. Student evidence and "I can" statements differ by grade level. For example, a third grader demonstrating leadership global competencies investigates the world by adopting and accurately restating an opinion, and at least one piece of supporting evidence from a source, in response to a global question. A fifth grader develops an opinion on the basis of evidence from a source in response to a global question. The complete set of global leadership performance outcomes is available on the Asia Society's website (see http://asiasociety.org/education/global-competence-outcomes-and-rubrics). The outcomes are designed to help schools integrate global competence throughout the curriculum.

In *Global Perspectives: A Framework for Global Education in Australian Schools*, Rae, Baker, and McNicol (2011, 5) describe five critical components of global learning and two dimensions teachers need to consider when helping students develop the values, knowledge, skills, and abilities needed to be a mindful global citizen:

- *Interdependence and globalisation*—an understanding of the complex social, economic and political links between people and the impact that changes have on others.

- *Identity and cultural diversity*—an understanding of self and one's own culture, and being open to the cultures of others.

- *Social justice and human rights*—an understanding of the impact of inequality and discrimination, the importance of standing up for our own rights and our responsibility to respect the rights of others.

- *Peace building and conflict resolution*—an understanding of the importance of building and maintaining positive and trusting relationships and ways conflict can be prevented or peacefully resolved.

- *Sustainable futures*—an understanding of the ways in which we can meet our current needs without diminishing the quality of the environment or reducing the capacity of future generations to meet their own needs.

- *Spatial dimension*—overlapping local and global; social and natural communities which describe interdependence, influence identity and ability to make change.

- *Temporal dimension*—connections between the past, present and future in the dynamic and changing world which influences identity and interdependence of people and their ability to respond to global issues.

Reprinted with permission of the Department of Foreign Affairs and Trade (DFAT), Commonwealth of Australia.

Each is discussed in depth and integrated throughout different subject areas for elementary and secondary education. Guidance is provided to implementing global learning in schools, including practicing active citizenship, teaching about the media (e.g., media literacy), using information and communication technologies, challenging stereotypes, addressing controversial and contentious issues, implementing inclusive classrooms, and more. *Global Perspectives: A Framework for Global Education in Australian Schools* is available at http://www.globaleducation.edu.au/verve/_resources/GPS_web.pdf.

The Association for Supervision and Curriculum Development (ASCD) provides educators with an online self-reflection tool called the Globally Competent Learning Continuum (GCLC). Educators can determine their own level of global competence by identifying where they place themselves on a matrix-based continuum. Teachers rate themselves nascent, beginning, progressing, proficient, or advanced based upon different criteria. Teachers evaluate themselves on the following elements:

- Empathy and valuing multiple perspectives

- Commitment to promoting equity worldwide

- Understanding of global conditions and current events

- Understanding of the ways that the world is interconnected

- Experiential understanding of multiple cultures

- Understanding of intercultural communication

- Communicate in multiple languages

- Create a classroom environment that values diversity and global engagement

- Integrate learning experiences for students that promote content-aligned explorations of the world

- Facilitate intercultural and international conversations that promote active listening, critical thinking, and perspective recognition

- Develop local, national, or international partnerships that provide real world contexts for global learning opportunities

- Develop and use appropriate methods of inquiry to assess students' global competence development

Used with permission from the Globally Competent Learning Continuum. Copyright 2018 by the Association for Supervision and Curriculum Development.

Educators can learn more about the dispositions, knowledge, and skills associated with the GCLC and access resources to improve their global competence. The ASCD GCLC is available at http://globallearning.ascd.org/lp/editions/global-continuum/home.html.

The U.S. Department of Education published the *Framework for Developing Global and Cultural Competencies to Advance Equity, Excellence and Economic Competitiveness* (U.S. Department of Education 2017). This framework lists four competencies: collaboration and communication, world and heritage languages, diverse perspectives, and civic and global engagement. This framework serves as a guide, showing how these competencies are developed over time and at various stages of education (early learning, elementary, secondary, and postsecondary). The *Framework for Developing Global and Cultural Competencies to Advance Equity, Excellence and Economic Competitiveness* can be accessed at https://sites.ed.gov/international/global-and-cultural-competency/.

What the World Teaches Us

Interest in global learning spread in the 1960s and 1970s as public support and concern for world issues increased (Bourn 2016; Pike 2013). Global learning incorporated themes of interdependence, the environment, discrimination, peace, and the future (Bourn 2016; Standish 2014). As technology advanced, interdependence among individuals, organizations, businesses, and regions of the world flourished. Today, the world is bound by its technological, environmental, economic, and political connections. The actions of one nation can significantly impact another, as well as the whole world. Understanding and communicating with diverse groups is critical in our global society.

Digital technologies make it easy to connect with diverse groups and share information across national borders. When participating in Web 2.0 environments (e.g., social networks), people describe themselves as multinational, multigeographical, and citizens of the world with friends from different parts of the world (Schachtner 2015). "In virtual space, it is not only diversity and cultural encounters that multiply, but also the opportunities for weaving lifestyles and identities from various cultural threads, making the need for unambiguous cultural classification obsolete" (Schachtner 2015, 237). This is not to say cultural understanding is irrelevant; on the contrary, cultural differences need to be recognized and respected in order for constructive conversations to take place. Ethnocentrism, or viewing the world from the perspective of one's own group, is narcissistic and counter to creating an interconnected, collaborative global community. Cargile and Bolkan (2013) share that intergroup ethnocentrism is reduced and cultural understanding increases when students engage in intercultural experiences, suggesting that students learn more from what they experience than what they are taught in a didactic manner. Global, intercultural experiences are real-world learning opportunities to see beyond one's ethnocentric self, cultural ideologies, and prejudices on the basis of one's place of birth and birthrights, or lack thereof. Global learning experiences can help individuals and groups question historical injustices, seek change, and see themselves as citizens of the world.

Global citizens are globally competent. Reysen and Katzarska-Miller (2013, 860) define global citizenship as "awareness, caring, and embracing cultural diversity while promoting social justice and sustainability, coupled with a sense of responsibility to act." Global citizens recognize that they live in an interconnected world, where choices and actions can affect everyone. People are connected socially and culturally via the media, Internet, travel, and migration; environmentally as a result of sharing the same planet; economically through commerce; and politically by means of international relations, systems of regulation, and issues concerning human rights (Ideas for Global Citizenship n.d.).

How Technology Can Support Global Competence

There are numerous ways technology can help educators develop globally competent students. In Chapter 3, resources are provided to help students and teachers learn more about different cultures, stereotypes, bias, discrimination, and inequities as a means to support social competence. This section provides additional resources to help educators and students examine these issues on a global perspective, as well as how technology can be used to help students and teachers connect with others to learn more about global issues, such as climate change, human rights, sustainability, and more. Virtual field trips and augmented reality (AR) are discussed as tools to help students explore locations and artifacts throughout the world. Resources for learning another language are provided. The section concludes with additional resources for teaching and learning more about global competence.

As mentioned, intergroup ethnocentrism is reduced and cultural understanding is increased when students engage in intercultural experiences (Cargile and Bolkan 2013; Krutka and Carano 2016). One of technology's greatest assets is its ability to connect learners throughout the world. Several free programs and apps, including Skype, Google Hangouts, Zoom, Facebook Messenger, and FaceTime (Apple), make videoconferencing an everyday, common phenomenon in many countries (Krutka and Carano 2016). There remain inequities in computer and Internet access, however, making it challenging for low socioeconomic students and those in remote areas to participate in on-line activities (OECD 2015). Barriers include hardware, cost, batteries, education, Internet access, and electricity (Hübler 2016; Krutka and Carano 2016). Organizations such as the Arid Lands Information Network and Computer Aid International are working toward removing these barriers, installing Maarifa Centres and ZubaBoxes in remote areas of the world (ALIN 2017; Wanshel 2016). Maarifa is "knowledge" in Swahili. Maarifa Centres are converted shipping containers equipped with computers and Internet access. Community members can come to the Centre to access information resources. Trained volunteers manage the Centres. ZubaBoxes are shipping containers transformed into solar-powered classrooms or Internet cafés for people living in isolated areas, including refugee camps. ZubaBoxes are named after the sun (Zuba is "sun" in Nyanja), are environmentally friendly, and act as a natural solution to the lack of electricity in many of the remote areas (Wanshel 2016).

There are multiple sites to help teachers connect their students with students throughout the world. These are listed and described in Table 4.3.

Table 4.3. Global Learning Projects Resources

Resource	URL	Description
Around the World with 80 Schools	http://aroundtheworldwith80schools.net/	A program designed to help educators contact other educators via Skype to set up classroom dialogues between students. Educators are encouraged to create a blog on the website to document their connections and share how videoconferencing is impacting student learning.
ePals	http://www.epals.com/#/connections	A website that makes it easy for teachers to connect with other classrooms. Global projects, pen pal exchanges, and more are available. Filters help teachers select an age range, country, subject, and more of interest.
Global Art Project for Peace	http://www.globalartproject.org/	An international art exchange program that promotes peace.
Global Education Motivators	http://www.gem-ngo.org/	A nonprofit organization offering a variety of programs and resources for teachers and students, emphasizing human rights and human responsibility.
Global Nomads Group	http://www.gng.org/	A nonprofit organization offering videoconferencing and virtual reality opportunities to engage with others from different cultures.

Table 4.3. (Continued)

Resource	URL	Description
Global Read Aloud	https://theglobalreadaloud.com/	An annual project that revolves around a selected book, connecting teachers with a community of educators in which to collaborate.
GlobalSchoolNet: The International Projects or Partners Place (iPoPP)	http://www.globalschoolnet.org/gsnpr/	A worldwide collaboration supported by GlobalSchoolNet and eLanguages that helps educators find global learning projects and partners.
iEARN: International Education and Resource Network	http://www.iearn.org	Helps facilitate student and teacher design online collaborative projects.
Kidlink	http://www.kidlink.net/	Promotes global dialogue among students through a variety of online project exchanges.
SchoolsOnline	https://schoolsonline.britishcouncil.org/	Helps teachers plan projects and find school partners; provides educational resources, courses, and funding resources.
TakingItGlobal	https://www.tigweb.org/	Provides global projects and communities, as well as educational resources for global learning and addressing global issues.

Global exchanges can be conducted at any grade level and address simple comparisons and data gathering to discussing and finding solutions to complex issues. For younger or lower-ability students, students may do the following:

■ Conduct a class survey about their favorite animal, food, or things to do, charting, comparing, and discussing the results with an international partner classroom. There are many online graphing programs available, including the following:

● NCES (National Center for Education Statistics) Kid's Zone Create a Graph (https://nces.ed.gov/nceskids/createagraph/). *This site also has a "Dare to Compare" activity where students can compare online quiz results to the average results in different countries and other tools. NCES collects and analyzes data related to education in the United States and other nations.*

● Math Is Fun: Make Your Own Graphs (https://www.mathsisfun.com/data/graphs-index.html).

● ChartGo (https://www.chartgo.com/).

■ Create round-robin or progressive stories among different global classrooms, dividing the story into five parts: beginning, build up, problem/dilemma, resolution, and ending (see *Travelling Tales* at http://bevansjoel.wixsite.com/travellingtales/about). Stories can be written and illustrated using an agreed upon authoring tool.

- Exchange, compare, and graph weather information and pictures with students from different parts of the world.

- Investigate how different types of pollution impact animals and the environment, connecting with students around the world to share local issues, strategies to raise awareness, and actions to take.

- Interact with students from another classroom in a different country to learn how education, resources, curriculum, requirements, and so on differ between their schools. Teachers can learn more about country educational profiles at https://wenr.wes.org/tools-resources/country-profiles.

- Share original poetry and stories, favorite recipes, favorite books, cultural traditions, and so on.

Older or higher-ability students may engage in projects that do the following:

- Examine concerns related to climate change, and partner with students around the world to share local issues, strategies to raise awareness, and solutions. Interactive models and simulations for learning more about climate change include the following:

    - Climate Time Machine (https://climate.nasa.gov/interactives/climate-time -machine)

    - Climate Interactive (https://www.climateinteractive.org/programs/world -climate/)

    - UCAR (University Corporation for Atmospheric Research) Center for Science (https://scied.ucar.edu/games-sims-weather-climate-atmosphere)

- Explore human rights—communicating with different international organizations and student groups to discuss the treatment of women, people who identify as LGBTQ+, people with disabilities, and other marginalized groups—and what steps can be taken to eliminate inequities. Resources can be found on Crosspoint Antiracism (http://www.magenta.nl/crosspoint/), an archived collection of links in the field of human rights. The Advocates for Human Rights website (http://www.theadvocatesforhumanrights.org/) is another resource, providing information for educators and students.

- Connect them with global partners to identify stereotypes and racism in the world, and find ways to reduce and eliminate ignorance, hate, and intolerance.

- Compare and discuss news headlines and other events taking place where they live.

- Create a band composed of worldwide musicians who practice and play together.

- Compare and discuss national food pyramids (healthy eating guides) and their relationship to obesity rates, the influence of food industries, sustainability, region and culture, and animal welfare. In addition, students may compare and discuss the power of advertising and how the media may or may not influence food choices. Resources for learning more about different food pyramids include the following:

- Healthy Eating Guidelines from Food Pyramids around the World: https://mic.com/articles/185100/healthy-eating-guidelines-from-food-pyramids-around-the-world#.p9KiZorCV

- Ethnic/Cultural Food Pyramids: https://www.nal.usda.gov/fnic/ethniccultural-food-pyramids

- What Food Pyramids Look Like around the World: https://www.mnn.com/food/healthy-eating/blogs/what-food-pyramids-around-world

■ Exchange and discuss clips of popular television shows and commercials, as well as discuss and compare how media portrays different genders, races, and stereotypes.

Students can use various technology tools to present their findings at Open House, a community event, or on a classroom website or social media platform.

In addition to classroom-based exchanges, technology provides students with access to virtual field trips and other online activities that can connect students with experts from around the world. Virtual field trips and access to online experts improve students' learning experience and academic performance, as well as reduce costs and accessibility issues associated with conventional field trips (Adedokun, Liu, Parker, and Burgess 2015; Greene 2015; Haris and Osman 2015). Using videoconferencing technologies like Skype, students can interact with experts to learn and ask questions about numerous topics. For example, Field Trip Earth (see https://fieldtripearth.org/social-media) provides students with access to wildlife researchers and other conservation experts. Microsoft Education features Skype in the Classroom (see https://education.microsoft.com/skype-in-the-classroom/overview) that provides numerous resources and collaboration activities for teachers and students. Resources include virtual field trips, Skype lessons, Skype collaborations, guest speakers, and global mystery games, courses, and much more. Resources are searchable by subject, age group, and location. Lesson categories include literacy and authors, STEM (science, technology, engineering, and math), geography and the environment, animals, history and culture, service-learning and social good, social and emotional health, and careers. Collaboration topics include geography and culture, reading and writing, nature and animals, and other subjects. Skype in the Classroom makes it easy to connect with other classrooms and experts, providing multiple collaboration opportunities and information on how to connect with verified guest speakers. Mini-courses, videos, and guides are provided to help educators learn more about how to use Skype in the classroom. Educators can earn *badges* for their work and become a Microsoft Innovative Educator. Certificates are available for student participation too. A Twitter search for #skypeclassroom will show tweets related to Skype in the Classroom.

Google Expeditions is another resource for providing virtual field trips. It provides students with a virtual reality (VR) experience of being at a given location. There are over 500 destinations available, with more in development. Google Expeditions requires a kit. Students need their own mobile phone, the Expeditions app, and a VR viewer (a cardboard headset, see https://vr.google.com/cardboard/). In addition, a tablet or other mobile device is required for the leader (guide), and a router that allows Expeditions to run over its own local Wi-Fi network is necessary. If peer-to-peer networking is not an option, a Wi-Fi hotspot can be created on a mobile phone (see https://support.google.com/edu/expeditions/answer/6335083 for more information). A speaker is optional. The teacher uses the tablet and chooses the role of Guide, the expedition, the focus, and points of interest. Students serve as the Explorers, following the Guide and focusing on what the Guide has highlighted. Teachers can pause the expedition to discuss or ask a question about a scene or point of interest. Students' screens freeze and will see an arrow directing them to the scene or point of interest. Teachers can draw on scenes to highlight areas, too. Expeditions are available on the app's home page by scrolling or by conducting a search. A list of expeditions is available on Google Docs too. Expeditions take place all over the world and include visiting Antarctica, Nepal, the New Seven Wonders of the World, Giants of the Sea, the Great Barrier Reef, Costa Rica, China, the Amazon, Cambodia, and more. College tours are available, as are tours related to various science topics (the nervous system, bacteria, climate change, etc.), works of art, events, and careers.

Google Expeditions AR uses AR to immerse students in 3D learning. Using their mobile phone, a selfie stick, and the Expeditions AR app, students can visualize and examine 3D objects in the classroom. Google's AR mapping technology allows 3D, virtual objects to be placed in the classroom, enabling students to walk around the objects, see the objects from all perspectives, get close to spot details, and step back to see the full object. Students can visualize the eruption of a volcano, the circulatory system, tornadoes, and DNA, as well as examine objects from all over the world. Students are able to interact and share their experience with each other as they inspect the virtual objects. More about Google Expeditions and Expeditions AR can be found at https://edu.google.com/expeditions/#about.

Technology can support teachers' and students' abilities to learn different languages too. In addition to translation tools (see Chapter 3, Table 3.6), there are many programs and apps that help users learn to speak and read different languages. Table 4.4 provides a list of language resources.

Table 4.4. Language Resources

Resource	URL	Description
Babbel	https://www.babbel.com/	Online and app language program. Speech recognition option. Free mini lessons. Monthly purchase plans.
Busuu	https://www.busuu.com/	Provides guided lessons, opportunities to speak with native speakers, and a global community of learners.
Duolingo	https://www.duolingo.com/	A free online and app language program that allows learners to set goals for language learning. Provides placement tests and an online community of learners. School option available, also, allowing teachers to monitor student progress.
Fluenz	http://www.fluenz.com/	A language-learning program available for 7–12 graders or adults. Includes ongoing assessments, scaffolding, and motoring options for teachers. Immersion opportunities in Spanish are available, also, with travel to Mexico City.
Linguistica 360	http://linguistica360.com/	Produces weekly language learning shows and educational materials. Features News in Slow, language learning through current events.
Rosetta Stone	https://www.rosettastone.com/	Online subscription, instant download, or CD-ROM options. Free demo. Monthly purchase plans.
WeSpeke	http://wespeke.com	Provides guided lessons as well as opportunities to speak with native speakers.

Table 4.5. Resources for Teaching Global Competence

Resource	URL	Description
Asia Society: Center for Global Education	http://asiasociety.org/education/lesson-plans-and-curriculum	Includes lesson plans and other resources to help build students' global competence.
Educating for Global Competence: Preparing Our Youth to Engage the World	https://asiasociety.org/files/book-globalcompetence.pdf	A book designed to help teachers prepare globally competent students.
Global Issues Network	http://globalissuesnetwork.org/	An organization designed to empower students to collaborate locally, regionally, and globally in order to create project-based sustainable solutions for shared global issues.
Global Oneness Project	https://www.globalonenessproject.org/	A library of free multimedia stories comprised of award-winning films, photo-essays, and articles, accompanied by lesson plans. Topics include climate change, water scarcity, food insecurity, poverty, sustainability, and more.
Peace Corps Education: World Wise Schools	https://www.peacecorps.gov/educators/	Provides educational resources to promote global competence, including lesson plans, activities, speakers, exchanges, and events—all based on Peace Corps Volunteer experiences.
Pulitzer Center K–12 Education Programs	https://pulitzercenter.org/pulitzer-center-k-12-education-programs	Offers lesson plans and other educational resources design to increase global awareness and encourage students to think critically about the creation and dissemination of news, to become better writers, and to develop their analytical and multimedia skills.
TED Talks: Global Issues	https://www.ted.com/topics/global+issues	A collection of TED Talks (and more) on the topic of global issues.

Resources for teaching about global competence are available too. Table 4.5 includes websites that provide resources for lesson plans, media resources, online experts, and more.

A Twitter search for #globalclassroom will show tweets related to the global classroom and #globaled will show tweets related to global education.

Studying or teaching abroad are additional ways educators can expand their abilities and global competence. Programs like StudyAbroad (https://www.studyabroad.com/) and GoAbroad (https://www.goabroad.com/) offer learning, volunteering, teaching, and intensive language programs throughout the world. Programs are available through the Bureau of Educational and Cultural Affairs Exchange Programs too (see https://exchanges.state.gov/).

The Internet and advancements in technology continue to make it easier to share experiences and work with people throughout the world to address global issues such as good health and well-being, quality education, inequities, climate change, sustainability, and peaceful and inclusive societies. The Internet allows marginalized groups to bypass the gatekeepers of traditional, centralized media, allowing alternative views and concerns to be voiced (Tukachinsky 2015). It is important that students understand that people have different perspectives on the basis of their experiences. Learning more about and cooperating with others from different parts of the world provide students with opportunities to see the world through others' eyes, as well as see how humankind is interdependent. For younger students, Morris (2017) suggests beginning with the concept that *people need each other*, having children share examples of how they depend on their family, how they and their family depend on the community, and how families and communities around the world depend on each other. Part of needing each other or being interdependent requires cooperation and nonviolent conflict resolutions.

SUMMARY

Since the mid-1940s, nations began working together to address issues confronting humanity, including human rights, gender equality, sustainability, climate change, terrorism, peace, and more. Interest in global learning continues to grow as public support and concern for world issues increases. Educational, government, and business institutions recognize the importance of global learning if students are to become globally competent.

Global competence includes the appreciation of different cultures, the ability to effectively communicate and exchange ideas with people from different backgrounds, and the proficiency to critically evaluate and analyze information and consider multiple perspectives. Global competence requires humility, divergent thinking, and technological literacy too. Students' success in our globally and digitally interconnected world requires that they engage in global learning activities so that they may develop global competence. Frameworks, outcomes, and rubrics are available to assist educators as they implement global learning in their classrooms. Multiple technology resources are available to help teachers too. These include websites for global exchanges and virtual field trips, Web 2.0 tools, translation and language programs, and Internet resources for lesson plans, media files, online experts, and learning more about global competence.

ACTIVITIES

1. Work with a partner and select one of the 17 sustainable development goals available at https://sustainabledevelopment.un.org/. Learn more about the selected goal and progress on the goal. What surprised you? What did you learn? How might you address this goal/topic with your students? Discuss your thoughts with your partner. Exchange findings and thoughts with members who chose a different goal.

2. P21's K–12 global competence grade-level indicators guide is available at http://www.p21.org/storage/documents/Global_Education/P21_K-12_Global_Ed_Indicators.pdf. Work with two or three other colleagues to create a unit for a specific grade level that addresses each of the indicators: understanding, investigating, connecting, and integrating. Use the Ch4. Resource Page: Global Competence Unit as a cover sheet to specifically address each indicator and the

Ch4. Resource Page: Global Competence Unit Rubric to guide the creation of your work. Present your unit to the class and share its significance.

3. Explore the Asia Society's website (http://asiasociety.org/education/global-competence-outcomes-and-rubrics) with a colleague. Take notes on why you agree or disagree with Asia's statements about why global competence matters (add your own reasons why global competence matters if you'd like), what the website and its links have to offer, and how its resources can support educators teach and learn more about global competence. Sit with a table group (e.g., six classmates) and discuss your findings.

4. Visit the online self-reflection tool at the ASCD GCLC website: http://globallearning.ascd.org/lp/editions/global-continuum/home.html. First, examine the full continuum to reflect on your own level of global competence. Find your level and identify areas of improvement. Next, discuss your analyses with your table group and share strategies of how to advance along the continuum. Explore the next steps—take action, reevaluate your level, and continue your efforts—presented on the website.

5. Work with a team of two or three other classmates and explore the global learning project resources presented in Table 4.3. On the basis of the resources, information, and sample projects available, choose or create a project to launch with your classroom. This can be a onetime event or ongoing, dependent upon your situation and project. If you do not have your own classroom, arrange for the project to be completed in one of your courses, as part of an after-school program, or within a classroom of another teacher. Make a recording of the event and share it with your classmates (if completed outside of class).

6. Work with a team of two or three other classmates and explore the Skype resources and activities available at https://education.microsoft.com/skype-in-the-classroom/overview. On the basis of the resources, information, and sample lessons available, choose or create a lesson to launch with your classroom. This can be a onetime event or ongoing, dependent upon your situation and lesson. If you do not have your own classroom, arrange for the lesson to be completed in one of your courses, as part of an after-school program, or within a classroom of another teacher. Make a recording of the event and share it with your classmates (if completed outside of class).

7. Work with two or three other classmates to learn more about another country's education system and its resources. Conduct research and connect with another teacher or other expert from the country to learn firsthand about the education system, including funding, curriculum, requirements, and so on. Create a multimedia presentation to share your findings.

8. Create or purchase your own VR viewer to use with Google Expeditions (see https://vr.google.com/cardboard/get-cardboard/#build-it) and download the app on your mobile phone (https://support.google.com/edu/expeditions/#topic=6334250). Next, choose and download a Google Expedition that you could use to enhance students' learning experience. Share your VR viewer and Google Expedition with a classmate. Discuss why you chose it and how the Expedition can be used to enhance students' learning experience.

9. Even if you already speak multiple languages, take the opportunity to learn another language or advance your current language skills by taking the placement test on Duolingo (https://www.duolingo.com/). Use Duolingo or other language tool (see Table 4.4) to advance your language skills and global competence. Write down and share your language-learning goals with your classmates. Work with a *study buddy* or group to help you stick to your goals. Report back on your progress in two weeks.

10. With a partner, review, compare, and critique two of the resources for teaching global competence in Table 4.5. Share your findings, reflections, and recommendations with your classmates.

11. Identify two technology resources not identified in this chapter that can be used to support global competence. Share these with your peers.

RESOURCE LIST

Asia Society

Global Competence Outcomes and Rubrics: https://asiasociety.org/education/global-competence-outcomes-and-rubrics

Association for Supervision and Curriculum Development (ASCD)

The ASCD Globally Competent Learning Continuum (GCLC): http://globallearning.ascd.org/lp/editions/global-continuum/

Books for Building Young Students' Awareness of Different Cultures

Kid World Citizen: https://kidworldcitizen.org/category/literature/

Partnership for 21st Century Learning Teacher Guide: K–12 Global Competence Grade-Level Indicators: http://www.p21.org/storage/documents/Global_Education/P21_K-12_Global_Ed_Indicators.pdf

What Do We Do All Day: https://www.whatdowedoallday.com/around-world-childrens-books/

Climate Change Resources

Climate Interactive: https://www.climateinteractive.org/programs/world-climate/

Climate Time Machine: https://climate.nasa.gov/interactives/climate-time-machine

UCAR (University Corporation for Atmospheric Research) Center for Science: https://scied.ucar.edu/games-sims-weather-climate-atmosphere

Food Pyramids from around the World

Ethnic/Cultural Food Pyramids: https://www.nal.usda.gov/fnic/ethniccultural-food-pyramids

Healthy Eating Guidelines from Food Pyramids around the World: https://mic.com/articles/185100/healthy-eating-guidelines-from-food-pyramids-around-the-world#.p9KiZorCV

What Food Pyramids Look Like around the World: https://www.mnn.com/food/healthy-eating/blogs/what-food-pyramids-around-world

Frameworks

Framework for Developing Global and Cultural Competencies to Advance Equity, Excellence and Economic Competitiveness: https://sites.ed.gov/international/global-and-cultural-competency/

Global Perspectives: A Framework for Global Education in Australian Schools: http://www.globaleducation.edu.au/verve/_resources/GPS_web.pdf

Global Learning Projects Resources

World Education News + Reviews Country Profiles: https://wenr.wes.org/tools-resources/country-profiles

(For further resources, see Table 4.3.)

Human Rights Resources

Advocates for Human Rights: http://www.theadvocatesforhumanrights.org/

Crosspoint Antiracism: http://www.magenta.nl/crosspoint/

Language Resources

See Table 4.4.

Online Graphing Programs

ChartGo: https://www.chartgo.com/

Math Is Fun: Make Your Own Graphs: https://www.mathsisfun.com/data/graphs-index.html

NCES (National Center for Education Statistics) Kid's Zone Create a Graph: https://nces.ed.gov/nceskids/createagraph/

Resources for Teaching Global Competence

See Table 4.5.

Round-Robin or Progressive Stories

Travelling Tales: http://bevansjoel.wixsite.com/travellingtales/about

Studying or Teaching Abroad Resources

Bureau of Educational and Cultural Affairs Exchange Programs: https://exchanges.state.gov/

GoAbroad: https://www.goabroad.com/

StudyAbroad: https://www.studyabroad.com/

United Nations

Sustainable Development Knowledge Platform: https://sustainabledevelopment.un.org/

Videoconferencing Tools

Facebook Messenger: https://www.messenger.com/

FaceTime: https://support.apple.com/en-us/HT204380

Google Hangouts: https://hangouts.google.com/

Skype: https://www.skype.com/

Zoom: https://zoom.us/

Virtual Field Trip Resources

Field Trip Earth: https://fieldtripearth.org/social-media

Google Expeditions: https://edu.google.com/expeditions/#about

Google Expeditions AR: https://edu.google.com/expeditions/ar/

Google Expeditions Support: https://support.google.com/edu/expeditions/answer/6335083

Skype in the Classroom: https://education.microsoft.com/skype-in-the-classroom/overview

VR Viewer: https://vr.google.com/cardboard/

REFERENCES

Adedokun, O. A., Liu, J., Parker, L. C., and Burgess, W. 2015. Meta-analytic evaluation of a virtual field trip to connect middle school students with university scientists. *Journal of Science Education and Technology, 24*(1), 91–102.

ALIN. 2017. Maarifa Centres [online]. Available at: https://www.alin.or.ke/. Accessed on November 4, 2017.

Asia Society. 2017a. Five reasons why global competence matters [online]. Available at: http://asiasociety.org/education/global-competence-outcomes-and-rubrics. Accessed on October 23, 2017.

Asia Society. 2017b. What we do [online]. Available at: http://asiasociety.org/education/what-we-do. Accessed on October 23, 2017.

Bourn, D. 2016. Global learning and the school curriculum. *Management in Education, 30*(3), 121–125.

Cargile, A. and Bolkan, S. 2013. Mitigating inter- and intra-group ethnocentrism: Comparing the effects of culture knowledge, exposure, and uncertainty intolerance. *International Journal of Intercultural Relations, 37*, 345–353.

Duncan, A. 2017. 10 activities to help your kids explore other cultures. The Spruce [online]. Available at: https://www.thespruce.com/teach-world-cultures-to-your-kids-3128861. Accessed on November 10, 2017.

Education 2030 Framework for Action. 2015. Incheon declaration sustainable development goal 4 [online]. Available at: http://unesdoc.unesco.org/images/0024/002456/245656E.pdf. Accessed on October 23, 2017.

Greene, K. 2015. Virtual field trips. *Instructor, 124*(4), 56–57.

Hammond, C. D. 2016. Internationalization, nationalism, and global competitiveness: A comparison of approaches to higher education in China and Japan. *Asia Pacific Education Review, 17*(4), 555–566.

Haris, N. and Osman, K. 2015. The effectiveness of a virtual field trip (VFT) module in learning biology. *Turkish Online Journal of Distance Education, 16*(3), 102–117.

Hübler, M. 2016. Does migration support technology diffusion in developing countries? *World Development, 83*, 148–162.

Ideas for Global Citizenship. n.d. What is global citizenship? [online]. Available at: http://www.ideas-forum.org.uk/about-us/global-citizenship. Accessed on October 27, 2017.

International Society for Technology in Education. 2016. ISTE Standards for Students [online]. Available at: https://www.iste.org/standards/standards-for-students. Accessed on September 18, 2017.

Johnson, D. W. and Johnson, R. T. 2014. Cooperative learning in 21st century. *Anales De PsicologíA/Annals of Psychology, 30*(3), 841–851.

Krutka, D. G. and Carano, K. T. 2016. Videoconferencing for global citizenship education: Wise practices for social studies educators. *Journal of Social Studies Education Research, 7*(2), 109–136.

Kuh, G. D. 2008. *High-impact educational practices: What they are, who has access to them, and why they matter.* Washington, DC: Association of American Colleges & Universities.

Mansilla, V. and Jackson, A. 2011. *Educating for global competence: Preparing our youth to engage the world.* New York, NY: Asia Society.

Mladic-Morales, B. 2014. 5 ways literature can teach global lessons in elementary classes. Edutopia [online]. Available at: https://www.edutopia.org/blog/literature-teaches-global-lessons -elementary-becky-morales. Accessed on November 10, 2017.

Morris, D. 2017. Rallying around the children of the world. *Childhood Education*, *93*(3), 264–268.

OECD. 2015. *Students, computers and learning: Making the connection.* PISA, OECD Publishing, Paris [online]. Available at: http://dx.doi.org/10.1787/9789264239555-en. Accessed on November, 4, 2017.

Partnership for 21st Century Learning. 2007. *Framework for 21st Century Learning* [online]. Available at: http://www.p21.org/our-work/p21-framework. Accessed on September 18, 2017.

Partnership for 21st Century Learning. 2014. *Framework for State Action on Global Education.* Washington, DC: Partnership for 21st Century Learning.

Partnership for 21st Century Learning. n.d. *Teacher Guide: K–12 Global Competence Grade-Level Indicators* [online]. Available at: http://www.p21.org/storage/documents/Global_Education/ P21_K-12_Global_Ed_Indicators.pdf. Accessed on October 24, 2017.

Pike, G. 2013. Global education in times of discomfort. *Journal of International Social Studies*, *3*(2), 4–17.

Rae, L., Baker, R., and McNicol, C. 2011. *Global perspectives: A framework for global education in Australian schools.* Australia: Education Services Australia.

Reysen, S. and Katzarska-Miller, I. 2013. A model of global citizenship: Antecedents and outcomes. *International Journal of Psychology*, *48*(5), 858–870.

Schachtner, C. 2015. Transculturality in the internet: Culture flows and virtual publics. *Current Sociology*, *63*(2), 228–243.

Standish, A. 2014. What is global education and where is it taking us? *Curriculum Journal*, *25*(2), 166–186.

Think Global. n.d. About global learning [online]. Available at: https://think-global.org.uk/global-learning/theory-of-change/. Accessed on October 23, 2017.

Tukachinsky, R. 2015. Where we have been and where we can go from here: Looking to the future in research on media, race, and ethnicity. *Journal of Social Issues*, *71*(1), 186–199.

UNESCO. n.d. Introducing UNESCO [online]. Available at: https://en.unesco.org/about-us/introducing -unesco. Accessed on October 23, 2017.

United Nations. 2015. Transforming our world: The 2030 agenda for sustainable development [online]. Available at: https://sustainabledevelopment.un.org/post2015/transformingourworld. Accessed on October 23, 2017.

United Nations. n.d. Overview [online]. Available at: http://www.un.org/en/sections/about-un/overview/ index.html. Accessed on October 23, 2017.

U.S. Department of Education. 2017. *Framework for Developing Global and Cultural Competencies to Advance Equity, Excellence and Economic Competitiveness* [online]. Available at: https://sites .ed.gov/international/global-and-cultural-competency/. Accessed on October 24, 2017.

Wanshel, E. 2016. This container brings internet to people in need, refugees in remote areas. Huffington Post [online]. Available at: https://www.huffingtonpost.com/entry/solar-powered-zubabox-internet-shipping-container-rural-areas-refugee-camps_us_5757155ce4b0b60682df2435. Accessed on November 4, 2017.

Young, D. 2016. What do globally competent students look like? Getting Smart [online]. Available at: http://www.gettingsmart.com/2016/02/what-do-globally-competent-students-look-like/. Accessed on November 9, 2017.

Ch4. Resource Page: Global Competence Unit

Group Members: _____

Grade Level: _____ **Topic:** _____

List how each indicator is addressed in your unit.

For example, for Understanding, a kindergarten unit may address: Students see that other people and communities have traditions that are different from their own. For Investigating, they may listen to, explore, and discuss a variety of picture books featuring stories from around the world; view short videos of how people live throughout the world; and so on.

Understanding:

Investigating:

Connecting:

Integrating:

Ch4. Resource Page: Global Competence Unit Rubric

Criteria	5–4	3–2	1–0
Goals, Objectives, and Standards	Unit goal(s), objectives, and standards are clearly defined, aligned, and appropriate for the intended audience.	Unit goal(s), objectives, and standards are provided and appropriate for the intended audience.	Unit goal(s), objectives, or standards are missing or are not appropriate for the intended audience.
Indicators	Each indicator is clearly addressed, aligns with the target grade level, and clearly supports the unit's goal(s) and objectives.	Indicators are addressed, align with the target grade level, and somewhat support the unit's goals and objectives.	Indicators are missing or do not align with the target grade level or do not support the unit's goals and objectives.
Outcomes	Outcomes are aligned with objectives, are measurable, and clearly build upon each other as students progress through the unit.	Outcomes are aligned with objectives and partly measurable. Outcomes do not clearly build upon each other as students progress through the unit.	Outcomes are missing, not measurable, or aligned with objectives.
Assessment	A variety of assessments are used to address students' different learning styles.	Three or four different types of assessments are used.	Two or less different types of assessments are used.
Timeline	The unit provides a clear, realistic, and complete timeline of what will be accomplished during the unit.	The unit provides a complete timeline of what will be accomplished during the unit. The timeline is unrealistic or not clear.	The unit does not provide a complete timeline.
Spelling, Punctuation, Grammar, and Tech Glitches	The content is professionally presented with no spelling, punctuation, or grammar errors.	The content contains some spelling, punctuation, and grammar errors but is still easy to follow.	The content contains numerous spelling, punctuation, and grammar errors.

Service-Learning and Project-Based Learning

OVERVIEW

Service-learning and project-based learning are active and problem-based forms of education that engage students in authentic and meaningful learning experiences that promote 21st-century skills. These high-impact educational practices engage students in real-world learning through community-based and constructivist learning experiences. Students learn by doing and working with others. Students have opportunities to express and apply what they have learned in multiple ways. Both service-learning and project-based learning activities support International Society for Technology in Education's (ISTE) Standards for Students, empowering learners to be knowledge constructors, innovative designers, computational thinkers, creative communicators, global collaborators, and digital citizens.

This chapter begins by discussing service-learning, followed by how project-based learning and service-learning are alike and different. Benefits, guidelines, examples, and how technology can be used to support service-learning and project-based learning are provided.

SERVICE-LEARNING

Service-learning can mean many things. In some cases, service-learning refers to fieldwork or field-based programs (e.g., student teaching, internships, clinical experiences) or volunteering in the community (Shapiro, Gurvitch, and Yao 2016). Students connect academic knowledge to real-world, authentic learning environments. Students learn by doing. Service-learning can also be described as working with community partners in an effort to analyze and solve problems, taking action to improve local and global communities (Kuh 2008). In the process, students use their voices, develop democratic citizenship skills, and become civically engaged (Montgomery, Miller, Foss, Tallakson, and Howard 2017). Britt (2012) categorizes service-learning into three categories: *skill-set practice and reflexivity, civic values and critical citizenship*, and *social justice activism*. *Skill-set practice and reflexivity* is based on the work of John Dewey and the progressive education movement and focuses on activities that help students develop competence and self-efficacy. Emphasis is on the student as a learner and connecting content with skills. Students learn by doing and reflecting. *Civic values and critical citizenship* is based on the democratic tradition of citizenship/civic education and focuses on values, social competence, and the student's role as a citizen. Service-learning projects that align with this category are designed to "raise awareness of and critical thinking about social issues and students' values and moral choices/responsibilities as societal members" (Britt 2012, 83). *Social justice activism* is based on social justice initiatives and critical pedagogy. Service-learning activities in this category provide students with opportunities to work with others to address oppression and other human issues related to societal injustices and balance of power. Students are seen as change agents. The outcomes or level of change within each category—*skill-set practice and reflexivity, civic values and critical citizenship*, and *social justice activism*—are cognitive, relational, and behavioral, respectively.

Service-learning is a process of both giving and receiving. For example, Kohr (2017, para 1) describes a service-learning activity where he challenged his third-grade students to "better the school community and solve a problem." Students were guided through an exploration and creative process that helped them find a real-world and meaningful project that would benefit their school. After brainstorming and discussing their ideas, students agreed to create a makerspace—a hands-on, collaborative workspace for making, learning, and exploring, designed to enhance students' critical thinking and creativity skills in STEAM (science, technology, engineering, art, and mathematics). Creating the makerspace benefited all students (including Kohr's third graders), teachers, and staff. The makerspace is currently being used for robotics, STEAM classes, behavior modification, and after-school clubs (Kohr 2017). Reed and Butler (2015) provide another example of a reciprocal service-learning project. After discussing how kindergarteners enjoyed bedtime stories and the impact of illiteracy, Reed and Butler (2015) asked their at-risk, urban middle school, nonreading students what they could do to help younger students develop literacy skills. The students agreed that they wanted younger students to love to read. The middle school students expressed how they were never read to and hated school. To help younger students learn to love reading and school, the middle school students decided to partner with an elementary school and read to the kindergarteners. Their service-learning project not only benefited the kindergarteners but also motivated, empowered, and improved the reading skills and attitudes of the middle school students (Reed and Butler 2015).

There are numerous benefits associated with service-learning projects. In addition to providing real-world and authentic learning opportunities, service-learning experiences develop students' citizenship skills; increase students' sensitivity to social problems; improve students' communication and cooperation skills; and increase students' motivation, sense of responsibility, and self-confidence (Ocal and Altinok 2016). Students involved in service-learning projects show improved academic achievement and attendance rates, as well as acquire 21st-century learning skills (Cooper 2014).

Service-learning projects can benefit students at all grade levels. For example, Montgomery et al. (2017) discuss how kindergarteners who participated in an arts service-learning project helped raise awareness about the educational inequities around the world and support for their underprivileged partner school in El Salvador. The project focused on the United Nation's Universal Declaration of Human Rights Article 26—The Right to Education. The students were able to recognize their own rights and educational privilege; engage in active citizenship; demonstrate awareness about global inequities; and express care, concern, support, and empathy for others. Fair and Delaplane (2015) share the benefits of an intergenerational service-learning project, where second-grade students made monthly visits to older adults. The students used journal writing to reflect on their service-learning. As time progressed, students' writing became more detailed and complex, and students demonstrated the ability to consider multiple perspectives, reflect upon their emotions, and realize that older adults could learn from them and they could learn from older adults, improving cross-generational understanding. Stereotypes were challenged, and students gained a better understanding of the needs of older adults and how to interact with people different from themselves. Scott and Graham (2015) conducted multiple service-learning projects with primary and elementary school students, including hosting a toy drive for a local hospital, having a clothing drive for a nearby homeless shelter, fundraising for a no-kill animal shelter, and teaching a lesson to a kindergarten class about diversity. Results showed a positive increase in students' empathy and community engagement. Middle school students engaged in STEM (science, technology, engineering, and math) service-learning projects demonstrated significant improvements in their academic engagement, achievement, civic responsibility, and levels of resiliency (Newman, Dantzler, and Coleman 2015). Projects included the building of an amphitheater, a water-testing project, and a cancer-awareness project. Service-learning projects can be global, as well. Foster, Cunningham, and Wrightsman (2015) share the results of U.S. high school service-learning projects that took place in Costa Rica. The researchers reported that students gained insights about themselves, a deeper understanding of others, and developed a heightened perception of the significance of intercultural awareness and global competence.

Service-learning projects are defined by the needs of local, regional, national, or global communities. Chosen projects should be aligned with the existing curriculum and standards and focus on the relationship between knowledge and action. Walker (2015) discusses the stages of a service-learning project: *Investigation and Inquiry, Planning, Action or Service, Reflection,* and *Demonstration. Investigation and Inquiry* are connected to classroom learning and expand to the local or global community, depending on the questions or issues being investigated. Students work collaboratively to conduct research and identify a project. The teacher's role is to act as a guide and facilitator. The teacher helps students focus on the goal of the service-learning activity and help them hone and reflect upon their ideas. Once the project is decided, the teacher integrates the curriculum within the topic the students have chosen. For example, Kohr (2017) taught prewriting strategies to help his students write a proposal to the school board for approval of a makerspace. Spreadsheet, design, measurement, and other mathematics skills were incorporated into the budget and blueprints of the proposal, and public-speaking skills were taught for the students' presentation to the building and grounds personnel and the school board. *Planning* involves student teams working together to developing community partnerships and communicating with stakeholders. This may include refining or expanding the original project idea. When students encounter obstacles in the planning/design process, the teacher helps students engage in problem solving, helping them to develop their critical thinking, creativity, collaboration, and communication skills. By focusing on the process, students learn to be resilient and cultivate a growth mindset (Brummelman et al. 2014; Dweck 2007; Kamins and Dweck 1999). Once the project idea and planning have been completed, students can take *Action.* At the end of the project, students reflect on the impact of the project, evaluating their service and their learning. In the *Demonstration* stage, students share their achievements and learning with others.

The RMC Research Corporation (2009), in association with the Learn and Serve America's National Service-Learning Clearinghouse, created a *K–12 Service-Learning Project Planning Toolkit.* In addition to containing material related to the five core components of service-learning described by Walker (2015) (i.e., investigation, planning and preparation, action, reflection, and demonstration of results and celebration), the *K–12 Service-Learning Project Planning Toolkit* provides a list of standards for K–12 quality service-learning. The topics and standards are as follows:

- *Duration and Intensity.* Standard: Service-learning has sufficient duration and intensity to address community needs and meet specified outcomes.

- *Link to Curriculum.* Standard: Service-learning is intentionally used as an instructional strategy to meet learning goals and/or content standards.

- *Meaningful Service.* Standard: Service-learning actively engages participants in meaningful and personally relevant service activities.

- *Youth Voice.* Standard: Service-learning provides youth with a strong voice in planning, implementing, and evaluating service-learning experiences with guidance from adults.

- *Diversity.* Standard: Service-learning promotes understanding of diversity and mutual respect among all participants.

- *Partnerships*. Standard: Service-learning partnerships are collaborative, mutually beneficial, and address community needs.

- *Reflection*. Standard: Service-learning incorporates multiple challenging reflection activities that are ongoing and that prompt deep thinking and analysis about oneself and one's relationship to society.

- *Progress Monitoring*. Standard: Service-learning engages participants in an ongoing process to assess the quality of implementation and progress toward meeting specified goals, and uses results for improvement and sustainability.

Indicators are provided for each standard. The *K–12 Service-Learning Project Planning Toolkit* is available at https://www.ffa.org/sitecollectiondocuments/lts_servicelearningtoolkit.pdf.

Although service-learning has many benefits, including improving students' social and global competence, Maryland is the only U.S. state that has it as a graduation requirement, in addition to the District of Columbia. Some U.S. states permit school districts to make service-learning a requirement for graduation, and other states provide credit toward graduation for service-learning (Education Commission of the States 2014). For graduation credit, Agrin (2017) notes that most school and district policies for service-learning include a specific duration for the project; the academic year the project must be completed (e.g., not before the ninth grade and by the end of the eleventh grade); whether or not the service must take place locally, nationally, or internationally; a list of activities that are permitted and not permitted; forms to be completed by the student(s); guidelines on how students need to present or reflect upon their learning experience, including how it connects to the subject matter being taught in the classroom; and a statement on how projects will be evaluated and graded. Schools or districts may want to appoint a service coordinator who oversees and assists with service-learning activities. A service coordinator is responsible for creating a plan for the school or district, acts as a community liaison, places and tracks students, conducts ongoing evaluations, assists teachers in developing new and adapting existing curriculum, coordinates media outreach, and researches and writes grants (Agrin 2017).

In some countries, service-learning is a requirement for admission into high school (Liu 2015). In other countries, high school graduation requirements require some kind of community service, research-oriented study, and social practice (Michael and Gu 2016). Several institutions of higher education require service-learning as part of the students' curricular experience, as well (California State University Monterey Bay 2017; Tulane University 2017; University of Wisconsin-Eau Claire 2017). U.S. News and World Report (2017) provides a list of institutions with exceptional service-learning programs.

Research shows that service-learning is beneficial for students at all grade levels, so it makes sense that students should not have to wait until high school or college to participate in service-learning activities. Service-learning is a high-impact educational practice that supports 21st-century learning. Service-learning projects provide authentic and real-world learning experiences, engage students in problem solving, increase students' empathy and community engagement, and build students' global and social competence. Learning is student centered, focusing on students' ideas, collaboration and communication skills, and interests. Curriculum is integrated to support students' learning and achievement.

How Technology Can Support Service-Learning

Technology can be used to support every stage of service-learning. In the *Investigation and Inquiry* stage, technology can be used to help students brainstorm, communicate, and research ideas for their service-learning project. For example, teachers can use online tools such as Mind Maps on GoConqr, Bubbl.us, and MindMup to facilitate students' brainstorming ideas. Apps such as Popplet, SimpleMind+, Kidspiration, Inspiration, and MindMeister can be used too. Students can track and share their progress using tools like Google Docs, Evernote, Moodle, Edmodo, or Project Foundry. Interactive whiteboard apps can be used to record and save students' work too.

Students can use the Internet to gather ideas and learn more about their proposed project. Educators can access sites such as the Environmental Protection Agency's (EPA) Community Service Project Ideas for Students and Educators website (see https://www.epa.gov/students/community-service-project-ideas-students-and-educators) to retrieve ideas and information for creating service-learning projects. Pinterest (https://www.pinterest.com) is another site that provides numerous resources—simply search for "service-learning" or "kids service-learning projects." Resources and ideas are also available at Character.org (http://character.org/key-topics/service-learning/), Edutopia (https://www.edutopia.org/blogs/tag/service-learning), and the National Youth Leadership Council (https://nylc.org/).

During the *Planning* stage, student teams work together to develop community partnerships and communicate with stakeholders. Videoconferencing (e.g., Skype and Zoom) can be used to communicate with partners and stakeholders; discussion forums, Google Docs, wikis, and other social media tools can be used to exchange, archive, and collaborate on documents. During the *Action or Service* stage, students can use technology (e.g., spreadsheets, graphing tools, databases, and Google Docs) to record, track, and document their work. Students can take pictures and make video recordings to incorporate into their final presentations (i.e., *Demonstration* stage), using the resources presented in Table 2.7 (Resources for Graphics, Animations, Audio, and Videos) in Chapter 2. Younger students can contribute to a class multimedia presentation or electronic book (e.g., Book Creator). During the *Demonstration* stage, students can choose technology tools and applications that provide them with the opportunity to express what they learned through words, pictures, video, audio, or a combination of different media. During the *Reflection* stage, students can use discussion forums to exchange and acknowledge each other's learning and share how the service-learning project personally impacted them. Students may also document and reflect upon their work using an ePortfolio (see Chapter 6). Advances in technology will continue to expand students' opportunities for presenting what they have learned.

PROJECT-BASED LEARNING

Project-based learning is similar to service-learning. Both are student centered, engage students in real-world problem solving, and teach curriculum concepts through a project. Differences include the following:

- Service-learning focuses on the needs of the community; project-based learning may or may not focus on the needs of the community.

- Service-learning is action oriented and impacts the community; project-based learning can take place entirely in the classroom.

- Service-learning is a form of project-based learning, but not all project-based learning activities involve service-learning.

In project-based learning, students design their own inquiries, plan their learning, organize their research, and use a variety of learning strategies (Bell 2010). The teacher guides students throughout the process. There are several phases of project-based learning (Bell 2010):

- First, students select an area of inquiry. For example, while studying different forms of pollution, students choose an area or topic of particular interest to them.

- Second, students decide on how they will conduct research on their topic and what materials they will need.

- Third, students choose how they will present their findings and what their project will look like.

- Fourth, students determine the audience for their findings/project— principal, parents, peers, and so on. The project must be relevant to the intended audience. For example, students may present their findings about pollution to the students of their school to raise awareness about the effects of pollution on their daily lives and future, as well as what they can do to help stop pollution.

- Finally, after students present their projects, they reflect upon and assess their work and what they learned.

To ensure student success, teachers need to help students establish due dates so that each phase of the project is finished in a timely manner. Formative assessment throughout the process can help students keep on track and provide teachers with opportunities to conduct mini lessons and address individual students' needs. Teachers and students will want to discuss criteria for the evaluation of the project before the start of the activity. The final assessment may be based on self, peer, teacher, and audience evaluations.

The foundation of project-based learning focuses on Dewey's theory of constructionism. Cognitive psychologists believe in the process of learning through the construction of knowledge. They assert that "people learn by actively constructing knowledge, weighing new information against their previous understanding, thinking about and working through discrepancies (on their own and with others), and coming to a new understanding" (Association for Supervision and Curriculum Development 1992, 2). These ideas, combined with social learning, are not new. Kilpatrick (1918) expressed the need to base education on purposeful acts and social activity, which he designed into his project method of instruction. Dewey (1929) stated that *social tools* (reading, spelling, and writing) are best acquired in a social context. Piaget believed that people try to make sense of the world and actively create their own knowledge through direct experience with objects, people, and ideas (Woolfolk 1987). Vygotsky (1978, 88) argued that "human learning presupposes a specific social nature and a process by which children grow into the intellectual life of those around them."

Professional organizations, such as the National Council of Teachers of Mathematics (NCTM), the American Association for the Advancement of Science (AAAS), and the National Council for the Social Studies (NCSS), continue to emphasize the need to engage students in constructivist thinking—decision making, problem solving, and critical thinking. Researchers (Gagnon and Collay 2001; Kaymakamoglu 2017; Marlowe and Page 2005; Shapiro 2003) define constructivist teachers as those who

- encourage and accept student autonomy and initiative;

- use raw data and primary sources, along with manipulative, interactive, and physical materials;

- use cognitive terminology such as classify, analyze, predict, and create;

- allow student responses to drive lessons, shift instructional strategies, and alter content;

- inquire about students' understanding of concepts before sharing their own understandings of those concepts;

- encourage students to engage in conversations with the teacher and with one another;

- encourage student inquiry by asking thoughtful, open-ended questions and encouraging students to ask questions of each other;

- seek elaboration of students' initial responses;

- engage students in experiences that might create contradictions to their initial hypotheses and then encourage discussion;

- allow wait time after posing questions;

- provide time for students to construct relationships and create metaphors;

- nurture students' natural curiosity through frequent use of the learning cycle model (discovery, concept introduction, and concept application);

- emphasize the process, including self-inquiry and social and communication skills; and

- are learners among their learners.

These teacher practices can help guide students in their understanding and support students' intellectual and reflective growth. Constructivist teaching practices increase students' intrinsic motivation and can help prevent teacher burnout too (Kaymakamoglu 2017; Zabihi and Khodabakhsh 2017).

In addition to focusing on constructive thinking and making teaching and learning more enjoyable, there are many benefits to project-based learning. Research shows that project-based learning increases students' academic achievement and learning permanence, fosters individual learner styles and abilities, promotes educational equity, improves students' critical-thinking skills and social development, and greatly benefits at-risk and minority students (Ergül and Kargın 2014; Holmes and Hwang 2016; Tasci 2015). Like service-learning, project-based learning is applicable to all grade levels and subject areas, and promotes 21st-century skills.

How Technology Can Support Project-Based Learning

Similar to service-learning, technology can be used to support students' research and inquiry process. Collaborative tools can be used to help students track and share their progress. Videoconferencing tools can be used to conduct interviews and research with experts (see Chapter 4). In addition, technology provides students with multiple ways of producing their final product. For example, students can create digital presentations, movies, e-books, simulations, and so on.

The process of creating digital content supports a constructivist approach, the foundation of project-based learning. Creating digital content provides a concrete and meaningful context for developing higher-order thinking skills, engaging students in the learning process, and inviting them to use technology as a cognitive tool (Edwards 2015; Ke 2014; Neo and Neo 2010; Piliouras, Siakas, and Seroglou 2011; Rhoades 2016). Digital content creation can help students learn how to develop concepts and ideas, design plans, apply what they learn, engage in multiliteracies, refine questions, make predictions, collect and analyze research, communicate findings, and solve problems (Bertacchini, Bilotta, Pantano, and Tavernise 2012; Neo, Neo, Kwok, Tan, Lai, and Zarina 2012; Rhoades 2016). Students begin to see themselves as authors of knowledge, collaborators, and active participants in the learning process (Connors and Sullivan 2012; Edwards 2015; Piliouras, Siakas, and Seroglou 2011).

Digital projects can be assigned using the DDD-E (Decide, Design, Develop, and Evaluate) method, as described in Chapter 2. In the Decide phase, student groups select an area of inquiry, conduct research on their topic, and select their target audience and digital creation tool. During the Design phase, student groups outline/sequence flowcharts; specify design, layout, scripts, and so on; and determine what materials they will need. In the Develop phase, student groups create or find the media elements necessary for their project and integrate the media elements into their chosen digital creation tool. Evaluation takes place throughout each phase as student groups reflect upon and refine their work. At the end of their project, students reflect upon their contributions and what they learned. Final assessment is based on self, peer, teacher, and audience evaluations.

According to Simons (1993), constructivist learning includes at least five components: active, cumulative, integrative, reflective, and goal-directed. Their definitions and relationship to the construction of digital projects are presented in Table 5.1 (Ivers and Barron 2015, 15). Gagnon and Collay (2001, 36) describe similar elements but include a sixth—grouping—noting that "small groups are necessary for students to move from personal meaning to shared meaning in the social construction of knowledge." Johnson and Johnson (2014) stress the importance of students working in small, cooperative groups, noting that cooperative learning is essential for meeting the challenges of the 21st century.

Herman, Aschbacher, and Winters (1992) also discuss the implications of aligning instruction and assessment with constructivist learning. Table 5.2 presents cognitive learning theories and their implications for instruction, assessment, and digital content creation (Ivers and Barron 2015, 16).

Table 5.1. Constructivist Components and Their Relationships to Digital Content Creation

Constructivist Learning Component	Definition	Relationship to Digital Content Creation
Active	Students process information meaningfully.	Digital projects allow students to be active learners by defining the content and creating the media components.
Cumulative	Learning builds on prior knowledge.	Digital projects allow students to connect current knowledge to new ideas through a variety of formats.
Integrative	Learners elaborate on new knowledge.	Digital projects offer environments in which students can create increasingly complex programs, as well as present current and new knowledge in new ways.
Reflective	Students assess what they know and need to learn.	Digital projects incorporate multiple levels of assessment at various phases throughout the design and development process.
Goal-Directed	Learners engage in purposeful learning activities.	When assigning digital projects, the teacher and students work together to define specific learning outcomes.

Table 5.2. Cognitive Learning Theories' Relationships to Digital Content Creation

Cognitive Learning Theory	Implications for Instruction/ Assessment	Relationship to Digital Content Creation
Learning is a process of creating personal meaning from new information and prior knowledge.	Encourage discussion, divergent thinking, multiple links and solutions, varied modes of expression, critical-thinking skills; relate new information to personal experience; and apply information to new situations.	Digital projects encourage knowledge construction and group efforts, stimulating discussion and divergent thinking. Media elements provide various modes of expression.
Learning is not necessarily a linear progression of discrete skills.	Engage students in problem solving and critical thinking.	Developing flowcharts and storyboards requires problem-solving and critical-thinking skills to "chunk" and organize information into linear and nonlinear formats. Students see how data relate to each other.
There are a variety of learning styles, attention spans, developmental paces, and intelligences.	Provide choices in task, varied means of showing mastery and competence, time to think about and do assignments, and opportunities for self-evaluation and peer review.	Design teams offer task options, allowing students to demonstrate their skills in many ways. The process of developing projects requires students to revise and rethink and provides students with hands-on, concrete learning experiences.
Students perform better when they know the goal, see models, and know how their performance compares to the standard.	Discuss goals and let students help define them (personal and class); provide and discuss examples of student work and allow them to have input into expectations; and give students opportunities for self-evaluation and peer review.	Rubrics, goals, and expectations for projects can be decided as a whole class without sacrificing the teacher's basic objectives. Sample projects can help clarify project expectations. The process of developing projects encourages self-evaluation and peer review.
It is important to know when to use knowledge, how to adapt it, and how to manage one's own learning.	Provide real-world opportunities (or simulations) to apply or adapt new knowledge; provide opportunities for students to think about how they learn and why they like certain work.	Digital projects support real-world learning experiences, plus it has the potential to enhance students' communication and metacognitive skills.

(continued)

Table 5.2. (Continued)

Cognitive Learning Theory	Implications for Instruction/ Assessment	Relationship to Digital Content Creation
Motivation, effort, and self-esteem affect learning and performance.	Motivate students with real-life tasks and connections to personal experiences; encourage students to see the relationship between effort and results.	Digital projects provide students with real-life tasks that they can connect to their personal interests and experiences. Digital projects serve as a visual outcome of students' efforts.
Learning has social components. Group work is valuable.	Provide group work; establish heterogeneous groups; enable students to take on a variety of roles; and consider group products and group processes.	Digital projects encourage cooperative grouping techniques.

Digital content creation can provide ideal learning environments for implementing project-based learning and a constructivist approach. Digital content creation encourages divergent thinking, multiple modes of expression, goal setting, critical-thinking skills, teamwork, opportunities to revise and rethink, and more. Students are active participants, constructing knowledge that is meaningful, applicable, and memorable.

Table 5.3. Resources for Project-Based Learning

Resource	URL	Description
Buck Institute for Education (BIE)	http://www.bie.org/	Resources for learning more about project-based learning.
Learning in Hand with Tony Vincent	https://learninginhand.com/blog/pbl-collection	A collection of project-based learning end products.
Learning Reviews	https://www.learningreviews.com/educational/free-teaching-resources/project-based-learning-lesson-plans-examples	A website with multiple resources and links for project-based learning.
Real Projects	http://www.real-projects.org/	An organization that provides support and resources for project-based learning.
TeachThought	https://www.teachthought.com/project-based-learning/a-better-list-of-ideas-for-project-based-learning/	A list of ideas for project-based learning, as well as other resources for learning more about project-based learning.
West Virginia Department of Education: Teach21 Project-Based Learning	http://wveis.k12.wv.us/teach21/public/project/Mainmenu.cfm	A searchable database of project-based learning activities.

There are many resources on the Internet that provide educators with support and partners for project-based learning activities. These are presented in Table 5.3. Chapters 3 and 4 present ideas for project-based learning too. These include global exchanges and other projects that can help students increase their social and global competence. Additional topics that may interest students include solar energy, climate change, virtual reality, augmented reality, pollution, engineering better medicines, space exploration, social justice, and so on. Students should be given as much autonomy as possible when selecting their area of focus, as long as they fall into the scope of the curriculum.

SUMMARY

Both service-learning and project-based learning are high-impact educational practices that engage students in authentic and meaningful learning experiences that promote 21st-century skills. Both support knowledge construction, critical thinking, problem solving, communication, and collaboration. Service-learning activities provide students with opportunities to develop their citizenship skills, increase their sensitivity to social problems, improve their communication and cooperation skills, solve problems, give back to the community, and develop 21st-century learning skills. Technology can be used to support each stage of the service-learning process: *Investigation and Inquiry*, *Planning*, *Action or Service*, *Reflection*, and *Demonstration*.

Project-based learning is similar to service-learning; however, unlike service-learning, project-based learning may or may not focus on the needs of the community and learning can take place entirely in the classroom. Service-learning is a form of project-based learning, but not all project-based learning activities involve service-learning. Project-based learning is built on the theory of constructionism. Students are involved in decision making, problem solving, and critical thinking as they investigate, research, collaborate, and communicate with others in the process of learning about their area of inquiry. Project-based learning increases students' academic achievement, improves students' critical-thinking skills, fosters students' social development, and promotes educational equity. Similar to service-learning, there are multiple ways technology can be used to support the phases of project-based learning. Collaborative tools can be used to help students track and share their progress, and technology provides students with numerous ways of producing their final product. Using the DDD-E process supports project-based learning when designing digital content.

ACTIVITIES

1. Britt (2012) categorizes service-learning projects into three categories: *Skill-set practice and reflexivity, civic values and critical citizenship*, and *social justice activism*. Work with a partner to provide an example activity for each category and describe why the activities align with their associated category. Share your examples and rationale with two other groups.

2. Discuss with a partner why or why don't you believe service-learning should be a high school graduation requirement.

3. Sit in a group with two or three other classmates and share what service-learning experiences, if any, you had as a K–12 student. Research and discuss whether or not your high school currently has a service-learning graduation requirement. If there are requirements, what are they? Discuss the service-learning experiences too, if any, you have had in college. If you are currently teaching, share what service-learning projects in which your class or school has participated. In what

ways have your service-learning experiences, or lack of service-learning experiences, impacted you? How do you think this will affect or has affected your teaching?

4. Discuss with a partner how your approach to teaching is aligned with or differs from a constructivist approach. In addition, examine how you learn best. Discuss how this aligns or differs from your teaching approach. How do you think this will affect or has affected your teaching?

5. For this project-based learning activity, place yourself into a group of three or four and decide on a relatively new technology innovation that you would like to learn more about. Using the DDD-E process, create a presentation that shares what you have learned about this new technology. The target audience for your project is your classmates. Use the Ch5. Resource Page: Innovation Project as a guide to help you create your project. (Other topics may be investigated; use the Ch5. Resource Pages of this chapter to guide your work, replacing "new technology innovation" with the topic of your choice.)

6. Work with one or two other classmates to explore and discuss the various project-based learning activities projects presented in Table 5.3. Decide on three projects that your group found most interesting. Share your findings, reflections, and recommendations with your classmates.

7. Identify two technology resources not identified in this chapter that can be used to support service-learning and project-based learning. Share these with your peers.

RESOURCE LIST

Apps

Concept mapping tools: Popplet, SimpleMind+, and MindMeister

Interactive whiteboards: ShowMe, Jot!, BaiBoard, and Educreations Interactive Whiteboard

Collaborative Work Environments

Edmodo: https://www.edmodo.com/

Evernote: https://evernote.com/

Google Docs: https://www.google.com/docs/about/

Moodle: https://moodle.com/

Project Foundry: http://www.projectfoundry.com/

Concept Mapping Tools

Bubble.us: https://bubbl.us/

Inspiration: http://www.inspiration.com/

Kidspiration: http://www.inspiration.com/Kidspiration

Mind Maps: https://www.goconqr.com/en/mind-maps/

MindMup: https://www.mindmup.com/

Project-Based Learning Resources

See Table 5.3.

Service-Learning Resources

Character.org: http://character.org/key-topics/service-learning/

Edutopia: https://www.edutopia.org/blogs/tag/service-learning

Environmental Protection Agency's (EPA) Community Service Project Ideas for Students and Educators: https://www.epa.gov/students/community-service-project-ideas-students-and-educators

K–12 Service-Learning Project Planning Toolkit: https://www.ffa.org/sitecollection documents/lts_servicelearningtoolkit.pdf

National Youth Leadership Council: https://nylc.org/

Pinterest: https://www.pinterest.com (search for "service-learning" or "kids service-learning projects")

Videoconferencing Tools

Skype: https://www.skype.com/

Zoom: https://zoom.us/

REFERENCES

Agrin, D. 2017. How to make service learning a graduation requirement. Asia Society [online]. Available at: https://asiasociety.org/global-learning-beyond-school/how-make-service-learning-graduation-requirement. Accessed on November 17, 2017.

Association for Supervision and Curriculum Development. 1992. Wanted: Deep understanding. "Constructivism" posits new conception of learning. *ASCD Update*, *34*(3), 1–5.

Bell, S. 2010. Project-based learning for the 21st century: Skills for the future. *Clearing House: A Journal of Educational Strategies, Issues and Ideas*, *83*(2), 39–43.

Bertacchini, F., Bilotta, E., Pantano, P., and Tavernise, A. 2012. Motivating the learning of science topics in secondary school: A constructivist edutainment setting for studying chaos. *Computers & Education*, *59*(4), 1377–1386.

Britt, L. 2012. Why we use service-learning: A report outlining a typology of three approaches to this form of communication pedagogy, *Communication Education*, *61*(1), 80–88.

Brummelman, E., Thomaes, S., Overbeek, G., Orobio de Castro, B., Van den Hout, M., Bushman, B., and Gauthier, I. 2014. On feeding those hungry for praise: Person praise backfires in children with low self-esteem. *Journal of Experimental Psychology: General*, *143*(1), 9–14.

California State University Monterey Bay. 2017. Service learning. *California State University Monterey Bay Catalog 2017–2018* [online]. Available at: https://csumb.edu/catalog/service-learning. Accessed on November 28, 2017.

Connors, S. P. and Sullivan, R. 2012. "It's that easy": Designing assignments that blend old and new literacies. *Clearing House: A Journal of Educational Strategies, Issues and Ideas*, *85*(6), 221–225.

Cooper, A. 2014. Learn by doing (good). *Instructor*, *124*(3), 23–25.

Dewey, J. 1929. *The sources of a science of education*. New York, NY: Horace Liveright.

Dweck, C. S. 2007. The perils and promises of praise. *Educational Leadership*, *65*(2), 34–39.

Education Commission of the States. 2014. 50-state comparison [online]. Available at: http://ecs.force .com/mbdata/mbquest3RTE?Rep=SL1301. Accessed on November 17, 2017.

Edwards, S. 2015. Active learning in the middle grades. *Middle School Journal*, *46*(5), 26–32.

Ergül, N. R. and Kargın, E. K. 2014. The effect of project based learning on students' science success. *Procedia—Social and Behavioral Sciences*, *136*, 537–541.

Fair, C. D. and Delaplane, E. 2015. "It is good to spend time with older adults. You can teach them, they can teach you": Second grade students reflect on intergenerational service learning. *Early Childhood Education Journal*, *43*(1), 19–26.

Foster, A.A.M., Cunningham, H. B., and Wrightsman, K. R. 2015. Using service-learning as a tool to develop intercultural understanding. *Journal of International Social Studies*, *5*(2), 54–68.

Gagnon, G. W., Jr. and Collay, M. 2001. *Designing for learning: Six elements in constructivist classrooms*. Thousand Oaks, CA: Corwin Press.

Herman, J. L., Aschbacher, P. R., and Winters, L. 1992. *A practical guide to alternative assessment*. Alexandria, VA: Association for Supervision and Curriculum Development.

Holmes, V.-L. and Hwang, Y. 2016. Exploring the effects of project-based learning in secondary mathematics education. *Journal of Educational Research*, *109*(5), 449–463.

Ivers, K. S. and Barron, A. E. 2015. *Digital content creation in schools*. Santa Barbara, CA: ABC-CLIO.

Johnson, D. W. and Johnson, R. T. 2014. Cooperative learning in 21st century. *Anales De PsicologíA/ Annals of Psychology*, *30*(3), 841–851.

Kamins, M. L. and Dweck, C. S. 1999. Person versus process praise and criticism: Implications for contingent self-worth and coping. *Developmental Psychology*, *35*(3), 835–847.

Kaymakamoglu, S. 2017. Teachers' beliefs, perceived practice and actual classroom practice in relation to traditional (teacher-centered) and constructivist (learner-centered) teaching (note 1). *Journal of Education and Learning*, *7*(1), 29–37.

Ke, F. 2014. An implementation of designed-based learning through creating educational computer games: A case study on mathematics learning during design and computing. *Computers & Education*, *73*, 26–39.

Kilpatrick, W. H. 1918. The project method: The use of the purposeful act in the educative process. *Teachers College bulletin*. Columbia, SC: Columbia University.

Kohr, R. 2017. A makerspace built by elementary students. Edutopia [online]. Available at: https://www.edutopia.org/article/makerspace-built-elementary-students. Accessed on November 28, 2017.

Kuh, G. D. 2008. *High-impact educational practices: What they are, who has access to them, and why they matter.* Washington, DC: Association of American Colleges and Universities.

Liu, T. 2015. Junior high school students' perceptions of service learning for admission to high school. *Procedia—Social and Behavioral Sciences, 197,* 75–82.

Marlowe, B. A. and Page, M. L. 2005. *Creating and sustaining the constructivist classroom* (2nd ed.). Thousand Oaks, CA: Corwin Press.

Michael, R. and Gu, M. 2016. Education in China. World Education News + Reviews [online]. Available at: https://wenr.wes.org/2016/03/education-in-china-2. Accessed on November 17, 2017.

Montgomery, S., Miller, W., Foss, P., Tallakson, D., and Howard, M. 2017. Banners for books: "Mighty-hearted" kindergartners take action through arts-based service learning. *Early Childhood Education Journal, 45*(1), 1–14.

Neo, M. and Neo, T.-K. 2010. Students' perceptions in developing a multimedia project within a constructivist learning environment: A Malaysian experience. *Turkish Online Journal of Educational Technology—TOJET, 9*(1), 176–184.

Neo, T.-K., Neo, M., Kwok, W.-J., Tan, Y.-J., Lai, C.-H., and Zarina, C. E. 2012. Promoting lifelong learning in a multimedia-based learning environment: A Malaysian experience. *Journal of Educational Multimedia and Hypermedia, 21*(2), 143–164.

Newman, J. L., Dantzler, J., and Coleman, A. N. 2015. Science in action: How middle school students are changing their world through STEM service-learning projects. *Theory into Practice, 54*(1), 47–54.

Ocal, A. and Altinok, A. 2016. Developing social sensitivity with service-learning. *Social Indicators Research, 129*(1), 61–75.

Piliouras, P., Siakas, S., and Seroglou, F. 2011. Pupils produce their own narratives inspired by the history of science: Animation movies concerning the geocentric-heliocentric debate. *Science & Education, 20*(7), 761–795.

Reed, P. and Butler, T. 2015. Flipping the script: When service learning recipients become service learning givers. *Theory into Practice, 54*(1), 55–62.

Rhoades, M. 2016. "Little pig, little pig, Yet me come in!" Animating "The Three Little Pigs" with preschoolers. *Early Childhood Education Journal, 44*(6), 595–603.

RMC Research Corporation. 2009. *K–12 Service-Learning Project Planning Toolkit.* Scotts Valley, CA: National Service-Learning Clearinghouse.

Scott, K. E. and Graham, J. A. 2015. Service-learning: Implications for empathy and community engagement in elementary school children. *Journal of Experiential Education, 38*(4), 354–372.

Shapiro, A. 2003. The latest dope on research (about constructivism): Part II: On instruction and leadership. *International Journal of Educational Reform, 12*(1), 62–77.

Shapiro, D. R., Gurvitch, R., and Yao, W. R. 2016. Video editing: A service-learning assignment in adapted physical education.*Journal of Physical Education, Recreation & Dance, 87*(2), 33–37.

Simons, P. R. J. 1993. Constructive learning: The role of the learner. In T. Duffy, J. Lowyck, and D. Jonassen (Eds.), *Designing environments for constructive learning* (pp. 291–313). Heidelberg, Germany: Springer-Verlag.

Tascı, B. 2015. Project based learning from elementary school to college, tool: Architecture. *Procedia—Social and Behavioral Sciences, 186,* 770–775.

Tulane University. 2017. Public service requirement. Tulane University [online]. Available at: http://tulane.edu/public-service-requirement. Accessed on November 28, 2017.

University of Wisconsin–Eau Claire. 2017. Service learning [online]. Available at: https://www.uwec.edu/sl/. Accessed on November 28, 2017.

U.S. News and World Report. 2017. Service learning. *U.S. News and World Report* [online]. Available at: https://www.usnews.com/best-colleges/rankings/service-learning-programs. Accessed on November 28, 2017.

Vygotsky, L. S. 1978. *Mind in society: The development of higher psychological processes.* Cambridge, MA: Harvard University Press.

Walker, A. B. 2015. Giving literacy, learning literacy: Service-learning and school book drives. *Reading Teacher, 69*(3), 299–306.

Woolfolk, A. E. 1987. *Educational psychology* (3rd ed.). Englewood Cliffs, NJ: Prentice-Hall.

Zabihi, R. and Khodabakhsh, M. 2017. L2 teachers' traditional versus constructivist teaching/learning conceptions and teacher burnout. *Current Psychology,* 1–7. https://doi-org.lib-proxy.fullerton.edu/10.1007/s12144-017-9610-z

Project Guidelines and Tips:

1. Place yourself into a group of three or four and decide on a relatively new technology innovation that you would like to learn more about.

2. Use the Decide, Design, Develop and Evaluate (DDD-E) process to create a presentation that shares what you have learned about this new technology. Assign group members roles, and remember the target audience for your project is your classmates.

3. Choose a presentation tool that you are comfortable with or has a low learning curve (PowerPoint, Google Slides, Prezi, etc.).

4. Remember to follow copyright and fair use laws.

5. Include a "credit" screen at the end of your presentation that lists your members and their roles, as well as any other credits necessary.

6. Arrange set times to meet so that each team member is able to participate in the production.

Day of the Presentation:

1. Make sure your presentation is accessible and ready to view.

2. Begin your presentation with a brief discussion of your DDD-E process.

   a. Share why you selected your topic and how you identified your team roles and presentation tool.

   b. Provide examples of your storyboards, or other materials/drafts of your planning stage, and how you researched your topic.

   c. Discuss the development process—what went well, issues, and so on.

3. Present what you learned about your topic.

4. Following the conclusion of your presentation, discuss the overall challenges, learning experience, and what you would do differently (if anything) next time while working on your project.

5. Presentations should be roughly 10 to 15 minutes.

6. Team members should complete and submit a peer evaluation of their group members and themselves. Audience members submit a review of the presentation too.

PROJECT RUBRIC

Criteria	5–4	3–2	1–0
Content	Overall, the content is clear, accurate, and appropriate for the intended audience.	The content is somewhat clear, but it is still appropriate for the intended audience.	The content is not clear, is inaccurate, or is not appropriate for the intended audience.
Spelling, Punctuation, Grammar, and Tech Glitches	The content is professionally presented with no spelling, punctuation, or grammar errors.	The content contains several spelling, punctuation, and grammar errors, but it is still easy to follow.	The content contains numerous spelling, punctuation, and grammar errors, or it is difficult to follow because of tech glitches.
Credit	The presentation credits the members of the team and borrowed sources.	Not all credits are provided.	No credits are provided.
Originality, Engagement, and Quality	The presentation is original and engaging. The quality of the presentation is professional.	The presentation is similar to others, but it is still engaging. The quality of the presentation is good.	The presentation is similar to others and is not engaging or looks like it was thrown together at the last minute.
Assignment Guidelines	The presentation follows the provided guidelines and instructions.	The presentation follows most of the provided guidelines and instructions.	The presentation does not follow most of the provided guidelines and instructions.

Group and Self-Evaluation

Submit the following:

1. Your name.

2. Name of group members.

3. Your team's strengths.

4. Your team's weaknesses.

5. What you learned about yourself in the process of working with others.

6. What you would do differently next time you worked as a team.

7. Your contributions to the team.

8. What you learned about your topic.

9. On a scale of 1 to 5 (5 being the highest), how would you rate your contribution to the team?

10. On a scale of 1 to 5 (5 being the highest), how would you rate your team member's(s) contribution to the team? (Provide the name and rating for each team member.)

Audience Group Evaluation

Group Name or Members: _____

How would you rate the group's presentation? (Place an "X" in the appropriate box for each category.)

Category	Agree	Somewhat Agree	Disagree
The content was clear, accurate, and appropriate.			
The content was professionally presented with no spelling, punctuation, or grammar errors.			
The presentation credited the members of the team and borrowed sources.			
The presentation was original and engaging.			
The quality of the presentation was professional.			

What I enjoyed most about the presentation was _____

_____

_____

The presentation could be improved by _____

_____

_____

Chapter 6

Research, Writing, and Information, Media, and Technology Skills

OVERVIEW

High-impact educational practices include practices that emphasize inquiry, critical thinking, frequent writing, and other skills that develop students' intellectual competencies and real-world learning (Kuh 2008; Watson, Kuh, Rhodes, Light, and Chen 2016). In today's global and technology-based workplace and society, information, media, and technology literacy skills are essential to students' research and writing success. Information literacy includes students' ability to identify, critically evaluate, analyze, and use information appropriately; media literacy expands students' awareness of how media can influence beliefs and behaviors, how to analyze and evaluate the intent of media messages, and how to create their own media messages; and technology literacy skills refer to students' ability to effectively and appropriately use information and communication technologies (ICT) for accessing, managing, creating, and communicating information (Partnership for 21st Century Learning 2007). This includes using computers, mobile devices, and social networks.

This chapter investigates the importance of research, frequent writing, writing across the curriculum, the development of ePortfolios, and how technology can support students' writing and research. In addition, this chapter examines how information, media, and technology literacy skills are essential to students' writing and research and reflects on what it means to be a digital citizen in our digitally connected, global society. The chapter concludes with activities that reinforce and extend what was presented in the chapter.

RESEARCH

The Association of College & Research Libraries provides a framework for information literacy divided into six frames (American Library Association 2015). Each frame includes a concept essential to information literacy, a set of knowledge practices, and a set of dispositions. One of the essential concepts is *Research as Inquiry*. As learners develop their inquiry and research skills, they:

- formulate questions for research on the basis of information gaps or on reexamination of existing, possibly conflicting, information;

- determine an appropriate scope of investigation;

- deal with complex research by breaking complex questions into simple ones, limiting the scope of investigations; use various research methods, on the basis of need, circumstance, and type of inquiry;

- monitor gathered information and assess for gaps or weaknesses;

- organize information in meaningful ways;

- synthesize ideas gathered from multiple sources;

- draw reasonable conclusions on the basis of the analysis and interpretation of information (American Library Association 2015, 7).

The K–12 Common Core State Standards focus on preparing students for college and career readiness in a technological and global society. The College and Career Readiness Anchor Standards are integrated throughout the English language arts (ELA)/Literacy standards and align with the skills associated with *Research as Inquiry*. Anchor standards are provided for reading, writing, speaking and listening, and language. One of the anchors provided for writing is *Research to Build and Present Knowledge*. Student outcomes include demonstrating the ability to conduct research on the basis of focused questions, displaying knowledge of the content being studied; collecting and assessing information from multiple sources, evaluating the credibility, reliability, and accuracy of the information and the source; organizing and synthesizing information from multiple sources, avoiding plagiarism; and analyzing and reflecting upon the evidence gathered (Common Core State Standards Initiative 2017).

Conducting research provides students with opportunities to ask questions, formulate hypotheses, analyze and evaluate data, and interpret their own observations. Student research may involve basic research, advanced research, or original research (Barron and Ivers 1998; Ivers 2003).

Basic Research

Students conduct basic research when they are asked to compare and report information from preselected sources. For example, teachers may provide their students with reviewed documents, articles, and websites and ask them to read, analyze, and discuss what they have learned.

Advanced Research

Students engaged in advanced research find and critique their own resources. Students analyze, evaluate, organize, synthesize, and interpret their findings. Students must have the necessary tools, skills, and strategies for finding and evaluating information. For example, when conducting research on the Internet, students should be equipped with different search strategies to help them limit the results of their searches. Many search engines have advanced search options, allowing users to search for all of the words in a phrase, an exact word or phrase, any of the words in a given phrase, or searches that exclude a specific word. In many cases, quotation marks can be used to search for an exact phrase (e.g., "rattlesnakes in Arizona"), and the subtraction symbol can be used to eliminate a word (e.g., rattlesnakes – Arizona). "Rattlesnakes in Arizona" will only return sites with the exact phrase "rattlesnakes in Arizona," and rattlesnakes – Arizona will return sites with rattlesnakes but will not include any sites with the term *Arizona*.

Many search engines have an optional *safe search* feature. For example, Google's Safe-Search acts as a parental control to help block explicit images, videos, and websites from searches.

Table 6.1. Search Engines Specifically Designed for Children

Resource	URL	Description
Kids Search	https://kidssearch.com/	Results are filtered by Google SafeSearch and additional filtering software.
Kiddle	https://www.kiddle.co/	Results are either handpicked and checked by Kiddle editors or filtered by Google SafeSearch.
KidRex	http://www.kidrex.org/	Emphasizes kid-related websites and uses Google SafeSearch. Maintains its own database of inappropriate websites and keywords too.
KidzSearch	https://www.kidzsearch.com/	Results are filtered by Google SafeSearch and proprietary artificial intelligence filtering algorithms. Available as an app too.
WackySafe	https://wackysafe.com/	Emphasizes kid-related websites and uses Google SafeSearch. Available as an app too.

Using search engines specifically designed for children (see Table 6.1) ensures search safety features remain intact. The safety features are not dependent upon which computer a student uses. Many schools have firewalls that prevent students from accessing inappropriate material. Unfortunately, filters and firewalls are not always foolproof. It is important to ensure that students understand the expectations of how they are to use the Internet and how to use it safely.

In addition, students must have the background knowledge and skills to recognize and evaluate the authenticity, reliability, and bias of electronic information. Students must understand that just because information resides on the Internet, it does not make it true. Students can assess the credibility of the information by looking at the source, the purpose of the website, sponsors, and currency and by triangulating the information.

Original Research

Original research goes beyond existing or advanced research. For example, instead of relying on existing research on web pages or in books to learn more about living in India, students perform their own original research by conducting e-mail, discussion board, or Skype exchanges with students in India; interviewing local India officials; engaging in virtual field trips; and so on. Global learning projects (see Chapter 4) provide numerous opportunities for students to engage in original research. Original research supports scientific-based inquiry and can be applied across the curriculum. Students determine what they want to know, conduct an investigation, collect evidence from a variety of sources, analyze the data, interpret their own observations, and report their findings.

Neuman (2011) describes the I-LEARN model for conducting, applying, and reflecting upon research. The steps include Identify, Locate, Evaluate, Apply, Reflect, and kNow (Neuman 2011, 2).

- Identify a problem or question that can be addressed through information.

- Locate information that can be used to address the problem or question at hand.

- Evaluate the information.

- Apply the selected information to the learning task.

- Reflect on both the product and the process of the preceding stages.

- kNow what has been learned so that it resolves the problem or question and so that it can be used to spur future knowledge generation.

The I-LEARN model can help teachers introduce their students to the research process, as well as develop and strengthen students' information literacy and critical-thinking skills, in grades as early as kindergarten (Tecce DeCarlo, Grant, Lee, and Neuman 2018).

How Technology Can Support Student Research

The Internet provides access to numerous resources. Search engines provide users with ways to refine their searches for information. Google Scholar (https://scholar.google.com/) can help older students locate peer-reviewed and other research articles. The OWL Purdue Online Writing Lab (https://owl.english.purdue.edu/owl/) is another resource for advanced students. In addition to writing assistance, it offers research and citation support.

Numerous online libraries exist where students can borrow and download e-books (see Table 6.2). Educators and students can access biographies, books on various science topics, children's books on different cultures, and more to help support the data-gathering process.

Web 2.0 technologies allow students to collaborate, share, and publish their research. Koltay, Špiranec, and Karvalics (2015, 88) describe this as *Research 2.0*, noting that Web 2.0 tools allow researchers "to create, annotate, review, re-use and represent information in new ways and make possible a wider promotion of innovations in the communication practices of research . . . by publishing work in progress and openly sharing research resources." As stated in previous chapters, technology provides students with multiple ways to collaborate on projects, share ideas, and present their work via Google Docs, Google Slides, wikis, discussion forums, and so on.

Technology can be used to capture students' research process too. For example, students can document their work by taking digital pictures and video clips, archiving and reflecting upon their progress as they develop an ePortfolio. Students can take advantage of text-to-speech options on websites to learn the correct pronunciation of scientific and other terms and use speech-to-text apps on their mobile devices to record their observations, interviews, and notes. Graphic organizers, such as Bubbl.us and Popplet, can be used to organize their research.

WRITING

Frequent writing and writing across the curriculum can increase students' writing quality, reading comprehension, and English language art scores (Graham and Harris 2016; Harrington 2018). Writing for authentic audiences and about something of interest can increase students' motivation and quality of writing (Festa 2017; Spanke and Paul 2015; West and Roberts 2016). The Common Core ELA/Literacy College and Career Readiness Anchor Standards for Writing discuss the need for students to write for a variety of audiences; use writing to demonstrate their knowledge of different subject areas; and dedicate significant time to writing, including opportunities to develop and strengthen their writing by editing, revising, and rewriting their work (Common Core State Standards Initiative 2017).

Table 6.2. Online Library Resources

Resource	URL	Description
ChestofBooks.com	http://chestofbooks.com/	Provides a variety of nonfiction books; topics include animals, gardening, history, health, and more.
International Children's Digital Library	http://en.childrenslibrary.org/	A collection of children's books that represent cultures and languages throughout the world.
Libby	https://meet.libbyapp.com/	An app that provides users with access to online audio and e-book collections via their local library. A library card is required.
Open Library	https://openlibrary.org/	An open-source library with over 2 million records; digitizes donated books; and authors can self-publish.
Project Gutenburg	http://www.gutenberg.org/	Offers over 56,000 free e-books; the first provider of free e-books.
Questia	https://www.questia.com/library/free-books	Provides over 5,000 public domain, classic, and rare books; search by title or author.
Smithsonian Libraries	https://library.si.edu/books-online	Features a variety of books in the public domain.
The Online Books Page	http://onlinebooks.library.upenn.edu/	Online books include more than 2 million works in various formats; search by author, title, and subject.

Writing across the curriculum provides students with opportunities to strengthen their intellectual and practical skills, demonstrate their subject-matter knowledge, articulate their thought process, and reinforce what they have learned (Firmender, Casa, and Colonnese 2017; Fisher and Frey 2013; Kuh 2008). For example, teachers can use math and science journals to incorporate writing activities that support metacognition, expand students' higher-order thinking and reasoning skills, deepen their conceptual knowledge, demonstrate their understanding, and improve their communication skills (Bernadowski 2016; Bostiga, Cantin, Fontana, and Casa 2016; Fulton 2017). As a result, students write more frequently; learn to write arguments to support their claims; write informative/explanatory texts to clearly articulate complex ideas; provide structure and detail to their explanations; interact and collaborate with others; plan, revise, and edit their work; gather and analyze information; and reflect upon their work—addressing each of the ELA College and Career Readiness Anchor Standards for Writing.

Although writing across the curriculum is considered a high-impact practice, teacher guidance and feedback are critical if the benefits of frequent writing are to be realized. Researchers suggest teachers provide focused and selective feedback; consider students' language ability and use language that is accessible to them; use constructive feedback, praising students' efforts, highlighting the positive aspects of their work, and addressing areas that need improvement; provide students with comments regarding the content of their work; and provide assessment criteria, including rubrics, before the start of the assignment (Agbayahoun 2016; Bradford, Newland, Rule, and Montgomery 2016). Providing prompts or focus questions and teaching and modeling the writing process, metacognition, and think-aloud strategies can enhance students' writing and understanding too (Bernadowski 2016; Bostiga, Cantin, Fontana, and Casa 2016; Fulton 2017).

In addition to teacher feedback, research suggests peer review is an effective instructional practice for teaching writing (Early and Saidy 2014; Loretto, DeMartino, and Godley 2016; Nicolaidou 2013; Woo, Chu, and Li 2013). Critiquing another's work provides students with insights into their own writing. In addition, students learn "how to share, discuss, and write about writing" (Early and Saidy 2014, 215). Researchers suggest educators teach students how to provide effective, constructive feedback, including how to be specific and how to provide suggestions and solutions (Gielen, Peeters, Dochy, Onghena, and Struyven 2010; Loretto, DeMartino, and Godley 2016). Reviewers should be provided with criteria for evaluating peers' writing, and students need to be taught how to interpret peer feedback (Loretto, DeMartino, and Godley 2016; Nicolaidou 2013).

How Technology Can Support Students' Writing

Technology is an integral part of the Common Core ELA/Literacy College and Career Readiness Anchor Standards for Writing. Standard CCSS.ELA-LITERACY.CCRA.W.6 states, "Use technology, including the Internet, to produce and publish writing and to interact and collaborate with others" (Common Core State Standards Initiative 2017). There are numerous writing, presentation, planning, and collaboration tools available to assist learners. Google provides many tools to support students' writing and collaboration, including Google Docs and Google Slides. Both are part of "G Suite of Education," a collection of tools to help educators increase students' opportunities to engage in critical thinking, communication, collaboration, and creativity. Graphic organizers (e.g., Bubbl.us, MindMup, Popplet, SimpleMind+, MindMeister, Kidspiration, and Inspiration) can help students as they brainstorm and organize their ideas. There are various other tools on the Internet that can be used to promote and support student writing. These include comic book makers, book creators, writing prompts, website builders, and animation programs. Table 6.3 provides a list of additional Internet resources to support student writing.

The Internet provides access to professional development opportunities for teachers and tools for creating writing assessments too. For example, ReadThinkWrite (http://www.readwritethink.org/) provides numerous classroom, professional development, and parent resources for reading and language arts. Rubric Maker (http://rubric-maker.com/) provides sample and customized rubrics. A search for "teacher writing resources" or "K–12 rubrics" will provide educators with numerous writing resources and rubrics.

Technology supports students' writing by offering spell check and grammar check, digital thesauruses and dictionaries, formatting and multimedia options, text-to-speech, and voice recognition and significantly eases the process of editing, revising, sharing, and publishing one's work. Technology can increase students' motivation, collaboration, confidence, and academic abilities and enhance their fine-motor skills (Clarke and Abbott 2016; Gerde, Foster, and Skibbe 2014). Writing scripts and recording their work for a multimedia/presentation program such as Powtoon or PowerPoint, a digital storyteller application such as Voki, or a screen recorder such as Screencast-O-Matic or Screencastify can motivate and help students practice their writing and speaking skills. For example, creating digital book trailers—similar to movie trailers—provides students with real-world learning experiences, purposeful learning, and opportunities to practice 21st-century learning skills (e.g., critical thinking, collaboration, communication, and creativity) and increases their motivation and enthusiasm toward learning (Festa 2017). Students can work in

Table 6.3. Internet Resources to Support Student Writing

Resource	URL	Description
Book Creator	https://bookcreator.com/	A resource for creating interactive, multimedia-rich e-books and more.
Make Beliefs Comix	http://www.makebeliefscomix.com/	A website for creating comic strips that includes writing resources for parents and teachers.
Pixton	https://www.pixton.com/	Students can create comic strips by clicking on and dragging characters, props, and speech bubbles into different scenes.
Powtoon	https://www.powtoon.com/	An easy-to-use multimedia, animation program.
Screencast-O-matic	https://screencast-o-matic.com/	Students can record their screen, themselves, or both.
Storybird	http://www.storybird.com	Promotes writing by encouraging students to use provided illustrations to tell a story. Stories can be shared.
ToonDoo	http://www.toondoo.com/	A resource for creating comic strips.
Voki	http://www.voki.com/	A tool that allows users to create a talking character.
Weebly	https://www.weebly.com/	A drag-and-drop website builder.

collaborative groups to create book trailers for their peers or younger students. The following requirements for a book trailer project are based on a checklist created by Festa (2017).

- The script is written at the appropriate level for the target audience.

- Images match the script.

- The actors speak clearly and at an appropriate pace.

- The trailer includes characters from the book, includes the setting, introduces the viewer to the plot of the story, and does not give away the ending of the book.

- The conclusion of the trailer is designed to ignite students' interest in reading the book.

Creating digital content is applicable across all subject areas, supporting students' writing through *All About Me* projects, science and other subject area reports, school and classroom newsletters, persuasive presentations, and more (Ivers and Barron 2015). Teachers can use technology to connect students with authentic audiences, as discussed in Chapters 3, 4, and 5, too.

INFORMATION, MEDIA, AND INFORMATION AND COMMUNICATION TECHNOLOGIES LITERACY

To succeed in the 21st century, students must be able to create, evaluate, and effectively use information, media, and technology (Partnership for 21st Century Learning 2007). This section defines and discusses information literacy, media literacy, and ICT literacy.

Information Literacy

Information literacy is the ability to access, evaluate, use, and manage information. This includes students' ability to conduct efficient and effective online searches, critically evaluate information and its source, use information correctly and ethically, and organize and synthesize information from a variety of sources. Educators can help students develop information literacy by modeling how to conduct efficient and effective searches (e.g., knowing how to narrow a topic, identify keywords, and how to narrow or expand searches) using online libraries and search engines like Google or search engines specifically designed for children (see Table 6.1). When evaluating website results, students should be reminded that all media—including television, radio, newspapers, and magazines—are platforms and distributors of facts, opinions, biases, stereotypes, misconceptions, and so on. Students must realize that anyone can publish information on the Internet and that evaluating all forms of media is critical. There are several criteria to consider when examining the intent and content of websites.

The intent of a website may be analyzed by looking at the domain name, the reason the information is posted, target audience, and layout (Ivers 2003).

Domain Name

An Internet address (URL) contains a protocol, a domain name, and sometimes a file location. For example, the URL http://www.fullerton.edu/academics/ contains the Hypertext Transfer Protocol (HTTP), indicating that the source is a web page; the domain name www.fullerton.edu, identifying that it is an educational site (i.e., it has the extension *edu*); and the file location *academics*, specifying that the user is in a directory called *academics*. Educators and students can begin evaluating a website by noting its domain extension. Common domain extensions include .com, .edu, .gov, .net, and .org. The domain extension .edu is reserved for educational institutions, and .gov is restricted to U.S. government agencies. Traditionally, the extension .org represents a non-profit organization. Sometimes, nonprofit organizations may strongly advocate a particular opinion, so students should take this into consideration when evaluating and using .org websites. The extensions .com and .net are opened to anyone. When examining a domain name, students need to ask: "Is there a likelihood of bias and special interests?" See Table 6.4.

Reason

Students should consider why the information is being posted on the Web. Every organization and person has their own agenda. Sometimes it is explicit, and other times it is hidden. Students should consider whether the sponsors' main purpose is to inform or influence. For example, students may ask: "Is the website designed to attract potential customers, donations, or membership to a cause or just to provide information?"

Table 6.4. Common Domain Extensions

Extension	Type of Institution	Level of Scrutiny When Evaluating the Site
.com	Commercial	High. Look for bias, what the site is promoting, and who is the source.
.edu	Education	Medium. Department and research centers are generally credible; however, student pages may not be monitored.
.gov	Government	Low. Information is considered to be from a credible source.
.net	Network	High. This extension is considered a "catchall" for sites that do not fit into any other domain suffixes.
.org	Nonprofit organizations	High. Some nonprofits, such as the American Red Cross and PBS (Public Broadcasting Service), use this domain suffix. Although their information may be credible and unbiased, there are other nonprofit organizations using this extension that may intensely advocate certain points of view.

Target Audience

Every website, just like commercials, has a consumer in mind. Students need to ask: "Who is the website for?" "Is it designed for children?" "Is it targeting educators?" "Is it geared toward a special interest group?" Students should consider for whom the information is written.

Layout

The layout of the information on the website may provide insight into the sponsor's intent. Students should determine whether the information is the main focus of the web page or whether it is in an obscure area, surrounded by unrelated content and links, advertisements, contests, giveaways, and so on. Questions to consider are: "Is the content clear and easy to navigate?" "Is the website an advertisement disguised as information?" "Do the graphics, links, and other media support the information, or are they unrelated?" "Are there other items on the site (advertisements, videos, flashing words, etc.) designed to distract users to other information on the site?" These questions will help students determine the intent of the website.

When evaluating the content of a website, students should consider the authority, currency, bias, and the validity and reliability of the information (Ivers 2003).

Authority

Students can assess the authority of information by determining if it is reviewed or refereed; identifying the author and his or her expertise on the topic; and verifying whether or not a bibliography or reference list is provided. Students may ask the following questions: "Have others verified the document?" "Does the document contain the author's biography and contact information?" "Is it possible to find additional information about the author?" "Are the author's citations accurate?"

Currency

Websites usually include the dates the sites were created and last updated. Students should look at the website's dates, as well as dates contained in the document, to verify the information's currency. Many websites are not updated on a regular basis, and others keep documents in archives for unspecified lengths of time. Students should check the timeliness of website documents on the basis of the publication date, not necessarily the date they were found on the Internet. Questions to consider are: "When was the site last updated?" "When was the document published?" "Is more current information available?"

Bias

As with all media, students need to be wary of biased information on the Internet. Some sites are designed to persuade rather than inform. Students must consider the point of view that is being expressed. They should ask: "Is the information written to inform or persuade me?" "Does the information reflect a special interest or specific point of view?" "Are stereotypes presented?" "Are different points of view considered?"

Verification of Information

Verification of information can be achieved by looking for inconsistencies in the information being presented, identifying whether evidence or examples are given to support statements or conclusions, determining whether the information is fact or opinion (or both), and recognizing what information is being withheld and why. In addition, triangulation of information—comparing findings among different sources—can help determine the validity and reliability of the information. Students may ask themselves: "Is the author consistent?" "Does the author present and consider different points of view?" "How does the author support his or her claim?" "Does the author present the whole story or just part?" "Have I verified my findings with other sources?"

Websites and other resources of information should never be evaluated solely on their looks. Looks can be deceiving, and anyone can publish on the Internet. Publishing tools make it easy to create appealing and professional looking websites and other materials. If the point of a sponsor is to inform, the information should be easy to find and clearly presented.

Even if the content is clearly presented, it may not always be correct. In addition to incorrect and outdated information, students must be aware of fact versus opinion, biases, and the credibility of the source or author.

In addition to examining the intent and content of websites, other considerations include the design and accessibility of the website. The design of the website may make it difficult to read, such as a dark font on a dark background or a cryptic or tiny font. Media, though well intended, may not be clear and may be difficult to access, distracting, or inappropriate. Accessibility includes whether or not the website meets the Web Content Accessibility Guidelines (WCAG). These are a list of recommendations created by the World Wide Web Consortium (W3C). The WCAG focus on ensuring that material on websites is perceivable, operable, understandable, and robust (World Wide Web Consortium 2017) and is compatible with assistive technologies. This includes text alternatives for images (e.g., alt text in HTML to caption an image), captions and transcripts for prerecorded and live-audio content, seizure-free environments (e.g., flashing content cannot flash more than three times in one second), keyboard accessible, and more. The complete list of requirements can be found at https://www.w3.org/WAI/intro/wcag.

Media Literacy

Media literacy is the ability to critique and create media. It "reflects our ability to access, analyze, evaluate and produce media through understanding and appreciation of:

- the art, meaning and messaging of various forms of media texts,

- the impact and influence of mass media and popular culture,

- how media texts are constructed and why they are produced, andhow media can be used to communicate our own ideas effectively" (MediaSmarts n.d., para 5).

Analyzing media includes understanding how and why media messages are created and for what reasons, examining how media can influence perceptions, values, and behavior. Chapter 3 provides examples of how the media plays an influential role on how viewers perceive gender, race, ethnicity, poverty, persons with disabilities, and LGBTQ+ individuals and how this contributes to stereotypes, bias, and unfavorable perceptions. As mentioned, educators need to be aware of the forces that shape students' attitudes and perceptions outside of the classroom, as well as how the classroom environment and curriculum materials impact students' learning, self-identity, and respect for others. Young children are especially vulnerable to media messages (Williams and Korn 2017).

The National Association for Media Literacy Education (2014) provides educators and students with key questions to ask when analyzing media messages. The questions are organized into the following three categories:

- Authors and audiences

  - Who made this?

  - Why was it made? What does it want me to do?

  - Who is the target audience?

  - Who paid for it?

  - Who might benefit from this message? Who might be harmed?

  - What does the storyteller want me to remember?

  - How does this make me feel, and how do my emotions influence my interpretation of this?

- Messages and meanings

  - What does this want me to think or think about?

  - What ideas, values, information, or points of view are overt? Implied?

  - What is left out that may be important to know?

  - What techniques are used to communicate the message?

  - How might different people understand this message differently?

  - What is my interpretation, and what do I learn about myself from my reaction or interpretation?

- Representation and reality

  - When was this made?

  - Where or how was it shared with the public?

  - Is this fact, opinion, or something else?

  - How credible is this (and how do you know)?

  - What are the sources of information, ideas, and assertions?

  - Can I trust this source to tell me the truth about this topic?

Sperry and Baker (2016, 183) note, "Media literacy models a constructivist approach to document-based analysis that asks the students to apply key content to a focused and complex analysis of messages, meaning, authorship, audience, representations and reality." Media literacy, however, goes beyond traditional, document-based media. Media literacy requires students to evaluate and become critical consumers of products and information, including television, radio, newspapers, magazines, movies, music, advertisements, comics, social media, text messages, videos, video games, the Internet, and more. Students need to be able to recognize different points of view, how media impacts our culture, and the impact media has on shaping people's attitudes and beliefs. For example, students can compare and contrast news stories posted by different media outlets and discuss potential bias. Students can assess the intent and impact of advertisements too, discussing how advertisements shape people's attitudes and beliefs. In addition, parents and educators can help children recognize and reject the effects of gender-stereotyped messages, such as Disney Princess media, to promote healthier, more realistic mindsets about gender and femininity (Golden and Jacoby 2017).

In addition to being able to critically think about the media they consume, media literate students are able to select and use appropriate media tools to effectively produce and express content. This includes adhering to ethical and legal obligations—part of their role as digital citizens. Students are able to use multimedia tools creatively, learning by doing, preparing them for a workforce that demands ingenuity, creativity, critical thinking, and the use of evolving forms of communication.

Teaching media literacy (media education) engages students in real-world issues; helps students understand how media can impact how they perceive different groups in society, deepening their understanding of identity, diversity, and difference; aids students' ability to see how media can influence their purchases, attitudes, lifestyle choices, and self-image; and teaches young students "to distinguish between reality and fantasy as they compare media violence and real-life violence, media heroes and real-life heroes, and media role models and real-life roles and expectations" (MediaSmarts n.d., para 5; National Association for Media Literacy Education 2007; Šupsáková 2016). Media education develops students' critical-thinking skills and awareness and is "a part of the basic right of every citizen in every country throughout the world; from the freedom of expression to the availability of uncensored and unbiased information reporting, it is instrumental for building and sustaining democracy" (Šupsáková 2016, 41).

Information and Communication Technologies Literacy

ICT literacy is the ability to ethically and legally use digital technology (including communication and networking tools) to research, organize, integrate, assess, and create information in order to function in a knowledge society (Partnership for 21st Century Learning 2007). *Knowledge work*, as described by the UN Educational, Scientific and Cultural Organization (UNESCO), has become the fourth and cross-sectional leading economic power of the traditional workforce (e.g., agricultural, manufacturing, and service), creating a *mindcraft* economy: "an economy that presupposes continuous learning within elaborate systems that combine human agents and intelligent ICT-based machines" (UNESCO 2005, 15). Educators can assess ICT integration within their schools and classrooms by examining the available technology on the basis of student and teacher needs; scheduled maintenance of and updates to equipment and software; goals and strategies for developing student ICT competence; professional development opportunities; and plans for monitoring, documenting, and evaluating desired outcomes (UNESCO 2005). In many cases, schools or districts create technology plans to guide the use of technology. For example, the California Department of Education provides a technology plan template, as well as an online technology plan builder, to support local educational agencies (LEAs) to establish clear goals and strategies to improve education through technology. The "California K-12 Education Technology Plan Template, Criteria, and Guiding Questions" includes five major criteria (California Department of Education 2015):

1. Plan Background: The plan should guide the LEA's use of education technology for the next three years.

2. Curriculum: The plan must establish clear goals and realistic strategy for using telecommunications and information technology to improve education services.

3. Professional Development: The plan must have a professional development strategy to ensure that the staff understand how to use these new technologies to improve education services.

4. Infrastructure, Hardware, Technical Support, Software, and Asset Management: The plan must include an assessment of the telecommunication services, hardware, software, asset management, and other services that will be needed to improve education services.

5. Monitoring and Evaluation: The plan must include an evaluation process that enables the school to monitor progress toward the specific goals and make midcourse corrections in response to new developments and opportunities as they arise.

Rubrics and additional guidelines are provided in the document. For more information, see https://www.cde.ca.gov/ls/et/rs/.

To address students' ethically and legally use digital technology, many schools require students (and parents) to sign an acceptable use policy (AUP). AUPs are designed to regulate students' use of the Internet and other technologies so that they do not harm themselves or others. AUPs typically include the goals of the AUP, definition of keywords, and the policies and procedures associated with students' acceptable and unacceptable use of the Internet and other technologies. The Children's Internet Protection Act (CIPA) is a federal law that requires schools and libraries that receive discounts for Internet access (e.g., through the E-rate program) to block access to obscene pictures, child pornography, or other harmful material to minors. In addition, school Internet safety policies must "include monitoring the online activities of minors; and . . . as required by the Protecting Children in the 21st Century Act, they must provide for educating minors about appropriate online behavior, including interacting with other individuals on social networking websites and in chat rooms, and cyberbullying awareness and response" (Federal Communications Commission 2017, para 3). Educators will want to address appropriate online behavior in their AUPs and with their students, including respectfully interacting with others, protecting their identity, and engaging in lawful and ethical practices. Educators can learn more about developing AUPs from the following resources:

- Rethinking Acceptable Use Policies to Enable Digital Learning: A Guide for School Districts (https://cosn.org/sites/default/files/pdf/Revised%20AUP%20March%202013_final.pdf)

- Webwise AUP Guidelines (https://www.webwise.ie/wp-content/uploads/2014/06/WebwiseAUPGuidelines-1.pdf)

ICT, information, and media literacy are applicable to young students too. In addition to its *Framework for 21st Century Learning* targeting K–12 students, the Partnership for 21st Century Learning created a framework and guidelines to support the integration of 21st-century skills in early learning experiences. The framework focuses on developing early childhood students' collaboration, communication, creativity, critical thinking, technology literacy, and social-emotional development. Technology literacy includes information, media, and ICT literacy. Outcomes include (Partnership for 21st Century Learning 2017, 17) the following:

- Understanding how tablets or computers are used to obtain information (including tools/technology like television)

- Judging between real and make believe (as seen on varying media)

- Using learned knowledge in new situations

- Asking how to find information, or using device/software creatively

- Using devices with adult consent

The guidelines address how children learn 21st-century skills—10 skills to help children build 21st-century skills—how to create the optimal 21st-century learning environment, and the importance of family engagement. Both documents are available at http://www.p21.org/our-work/elf.

ePORTFOLIOS

Research, writing, and information, media, and ICT literacy provide the foundation for the development of ePortfolios. ePortfolios require students to gather, evaluate, and organize information in meaningful ways; synthesize ideas gathered from multiple sources; and present and demonstrate their knowledge. ePortfolios provide students the opportunity to document, demonstrate, develop, revise, and reflect upon their learning, as well as support the growth of students' digital identity (Cooper 2014). ePortfolios can be used to increase awareness of self and others, set goals on the basis of personal interests and values, establish pathways and strategies for achieving goals, and shape students' education and career plans (Buyarski et al. 2015). ePortfolios can be a collection of work and reflections over an extended period of time (e.g., a student's college, high school, or other educational experience) or a product based on a specific assignment. For example, students may be asked to create a class or individual ePortfolio as they learn about the Industrial Revolution, American symbols, or animal habits.

Compared to paper-based portfolios, ePortfolios provide students the opportunity to collect, create, present, and reflect upon their work using a variety of digital media (video, audio, animation, graphics, etc.), addressing multimodalities of learning and ways to demonstrate knowledge. ePortfolios can be created using tools like Weebly, Wix, Digication, Google Sites, PortfolioGen, Kidblog, and Edublogs. SeeSaw, a digital portfolio system for schools, is another option. Schools may have other systems (Blackboard, Moodle, Canvas, etc.) that provide students with options for creating ePortfolios too. Unlike paper-based portfolios, ePortfolios can be easily shared and updated. Portfolium, a platform for students to showcase their projects, coursework, and skills, is specifically designed to allow recruiters and employers to search for potential employees or interns. As society continues to rely more heavily on digital communication, it is important that students (and educators) learn to demonstrate and share their abilities through multimedia platforms such as ePortfolios. Competency-based hiring is on the rise (Craig and Blivin 2016); the Association of American Colleges & Universities reports that 83 percent of employers say ePortfolios are useful to them, and 93 percent say that "a candidate's demonstrated capacity to think critically, communicate clearly, and solve complex problems is more important than their undergraduate major" (Hart Research Associates 2013, para 4).

As with other software, educators need to evaluate which tools are most appropriate for the needs and developmental level of their students. Brown (2015) suggests educators consider the *affordances* of the software or platform (If video is needed, how well does it store and deliver the videos? Does the program provide opportunities for collaboration?); *usability* (How easy is it for students to use?); *accessibility* (Can it be accessed through the Internet, and is the content accessible to everyone, including those with visual or audio disabilities?); and the *cost and help* needed to run the program (Is it free? Does it require a subscription and require on-campus staff to maintain the software?). Educators should consider limitations of the platform as well (storage capacity, number of students who can have access, if advertisements are on the screen, etc.).

Most online programs provide templates and other support for creating ePortfolios. General guidelines for assigning and developing ePortfolios include the following:

Assigning (teacher)

- Defining the objective or purpose of the ePortfolio

- Identifying the learning outcomes (e.g., standards)

- Providing students with a list of expectations, timelines, and criteria

- Describing how the ePortfolio will be monitored over time

- Discussing the feedback, revision, and final evaluation process

Developing (student)

- Generating or gathering material to include in the ePortfolio based on the learning objective

- Selecting, organizing, and linking items from the gathered materials that demonstrate learning over time, eliminating excess, repetitiveness, or irrelevant information

- Reflecting on the selected work, demonstrating mastery of the standard

- Discussing the process, learning, and future goals with the teacher and peers

- Sharing and showcasing final work

The assessment of the ePortfolio should be based on how well the student demonstrated achievement of the learning goal or standard, as well as met the list of expectations, timelines, and criteria.

DIGITAL CITIZENSHIP

The concept of *digital citizen* is multifaceted and continues to evolve with the advancement of technology. Researchers continue to explore ways to define what it means to be a digital citizen, developing methods for measuring digital citizenship (Choi, Glassman, and Cristol 2017; Isman and Canan Gungoren 2013; Jones and Mitchell 2016), examining the implications of digital identity under international law (Sullivan 2016), and creating frameworks and guidelines for developing digital citizens (Common Sense Education 2016; Ribble 2014). Digital citizenship can be defined as the legal, ethical, and safe use of technology; a way of thinking, being, and acting online; and safe and responsible online behavior (Common Sense Media n.d.; ISTE 2016; Jones and Mitchell 2016). Ribble (2014) identifies three categories and defines nine separate digital citizen topics. These include digital access, digital etiquette, and digital law (topics under the category of *Respect*); digital communication, digital literacy, and digital commerce (topics under the category of *Educate*); and digital rights and responsibilities, digital safety and security, and digital health and wellness (topics under the category of *Protect*). Topics in the category of *Respect* focus on equity, treating others appropriately, and respecting the work of others. Topics in the category of *Educate* highlight the significance of teaching students how to use communication tools wisely, how to learn in a digital world, and how to be an informed, online consumer. Topics in the category of *Protect* emphasize the importance of ensuring privacy and free speech, keeping students safe from cyberattacks, and minimizing the harmful physical and psychological effects that can result from being addicted to technology.

Common Sense Education (2016) identifies the following categories for teaching digital citizenship: *Privacy and Security, Digital Footprint and Reputation, Self-Image and Identity, Creative Credit and Copyright, Relationships and Communication, Information Literacy, Cyberbullying and Digital Drama*, and *Internet Safety*. In *Privacy and Security*, students learn how to keep their online information secure, create strong passwords, and recognize identity thieves and phishing. In *Digital Footprint and Reputation*, students focus on protecting their privacy and respecting the privacy of others and to *self-reflect* before they *self-reveal*, understanding that the digital world is permanent. Students reflect upon their online and off-line identities in *Self-Image and Identity* and think about their responsibilities and rights as creators, including plagiarism and piracy in *Creative Credit and Copyright*. In *Relationships and Communication*, students examine their interpersonal and intrapersonal skills as they relate to effective online communication and communities. Students learn to find, evaluate, and use information effectively in *Information Literacy* and how their actions, including cyberbullying, can impact others in *Cyberbullying and Digital Drama*. Students learn how to safely navigate and use the Internet in *Internet Safety*.

Jones and Mitchell (2016) believe digital literacy education (Internet and computer technical skills) and cyberbullying prevention should be separate from digital citizenship education. The researchers define digital citizen education as "using Internet resources to have youth (1) practice respectful and tolerant behavior towards others and (2) increase civic engagement activities" (Jones and Mitchell 2016, 2065). The researchers see the Internet as a way to help students practice positive social skills and engage with their community. Hollandsworth, Donovan, and Welch (2017) state that digital education in schools has not changed much, noting that emphasis continues to be on plagiarism, copyright, evaluating electronic information, and protecting personal information.

Engaging and preparing students for a global, digitally connected society requires educators to step beyond digital literacy skills. As Jones and Mitchell (2016) and other researchers suggest, we need to prepare our students to be socially and globally competent, collaborative learners, and critical consumers of information. While ensuring students remain safe and practice ethical and responsible behavior on the Internet, teaching our students to be digital citizens is similar to teaching them how to be collaborative, ethical, and responsible global citizens. Online and off-line, the world is their community.

SUMMARY

High-impact educational practices include research, writing, and the development of ePortfolios. In today's technology-based society, students are engaged in digital research, writing, and communication, reinforcing the need for students to develop information, media, and ICT literacy skills. In addition, students need to recognize their roles and responsibilities as digital citizens in our global and digitally connected society.

Research reinforces students' inquiry and critical-thinking skills. Students may engage in basic, advanced, or original research. There are multiple ways technology can support student research, including providing an abundance of resources on the Internet; safe search engines to protect students from explicit images, videos, and websites; and tools for collaboration, sharing, and publishing their research.

Frequent writing, writing across the curriculum, and writing for different audiences help to increase students' writing quality, motivation, and reading comprehension. Writing allows students to articulate their thought process and reinforces what they have learned. Peer review and teacher feedback are effective instructional practices for teaching writing. Technology significantly eases the process of editing, revising, sharing, and publishing one's work. In addition, technology programs offer spell check and grammar check, digital thesauruses and dictionaries, formatting and multimedia options, text-to-speech, voice recognition, and more. Presentation, planning, and collaboration tools are available to assist learners, and technology provides numerous opportunities for students to exchange work with authentic audiences, providing real-world learning experiences and increasing students' motivation to write.

Information literacy, media literacy, and ICT literacy are skills students need to succeed in a digital and global society. Information literacy is the ability to access, evaluate, use, and manage information. Media literacy is the ability to critique and create media. ICT literacy is the ability to ethically and legally use digital technology (including communication and networking tools) to research, organize, integrate, assess, and create information in order to function in a knowledge society. Information literacy, media literacy, and ICT literacy are critical skills for research and writing, as well as the development of ePortfolios. ePortfolios require students to gather, evaluate, and organize information in meaningful ways, synthesize ideas gathered from multiple sources, and present and demonstrate their knowledge.

The advancement, accessibility, and increased integration of technology in today's digital and global society require students to reflect upon their role and responsibility as a digital citizen. Being a digital citizen is multifaceted and continues to evolve with the advancement of technology. As a result, it is important that we align our use of technology with high-impact educational practices.

ACTIVITIES

1. Choose an educational technology topic/issue of interest, and write a five- to seven-page research paper that reflects your findings. Use reputable and current resources to support your work. Include citations and a list of references.

2. With a partner, review, compare, and critique two of the search engines specifically designed for children in Table 6.1. Share your findings, reflections, and recommendations with your classmates.

3. With a partner, review, compare, and critique two of the Internet resources to support student writing in Table 6.2. Share your findings, reflections, and recommendations with your classmates.

4. Use the Ch6. Resource Page: Website Evaluation Checklist to evaluate two websites that are designed for student research. Each website should have its own Website Evaluation Checklist. Look for websites that are content specific. For example, if you want your students to conduct research to learn more about Abraham Lincoln, find websites that provide content related to Abraham Lincoln, and evaluate the sites to see if they are appropriate for your students. This is a _Basic Research_ activity, where the teacher finds preselected resources for his or her students' research projects. Remember you are looking for websites that deliver content, not games, quizzes, activities, links, or teacher resources. Your search for and evaluation of two content-specific websites may not turn up two _good_ sites for this activity but your evaluation of the websites will help you identify criteria to consider when choosing websites for students' basic research. Later, using what you learned, you can teach your students how to evaluate websites. Share your findings with your classmates.

5. Šupsáková (2016, 41) states that media education is "a part of the basic right of every citizen in every country throughout the world; from the freedom of expression to the availability of uncensored and unbiased information reporting, it is instrumental for building and sustaining democracy." Do you agree or disagree? Share your rationale with a partner.

6. Work with two or three of your peers to select a grade level, and develop a unit on media literacy.

7. Examine your school's AUP and technology plan. If you are not currently teaching, you can access these documents on a local school or district website. How does the AUP compare to Rethinking Acceptable Use Policies to Enable Digital Learning: A Guide for School Districts or the Webwise AUP Guidelines? How does the technology plan: (1) Guide the LEA's use of education technology? (2) Establish clear goals and realistic strategy for using telecommunications and information technology to improve education services? (3) Provide a professional development strategy to ensure that the staff understand how to use new technologies to improve education services? (4) Assess telecommunication services, hardware, software, asset management, and other services that will be needed to improve education services? (5) Monitor progress toward the specific goals of the technology plan and make midcourse corrections in response to new developments and opportunities as they arise? Share your findings and recommendations with your classmates.

8. Create an ePortfolio that reflects your work as a professional educator. Include a professional picture of yourself; your educational philosophy; résumé; sample work (these could be pictures); special talents, accomplishments, or interests; and any other information you deem relevant to marketing yourself (recommendations, awards, related work experience, etc.). Make sure your portfolio is free from spelling, grammar, and punctuation errors; is clear and easy to navigate; is accurate and up-to-date; and presents you as a professional.

9. Describe what it means to be a digital citizen. How can we best prepare our students to be digital citizens? Support your rationale and share your thoughts with your classmates.

10. Identify two technology resources not identified in this chapter that can be used to support research, writing, and information, media, and technology skills. Share these with your peers.

RESOURCE LIST

Acceptable Use Policies and Technology Plan Resources

California K-12 Education Technology Plan Template, Criteria, and Guiding Questions: https://www.cde.ca.gov/ls/et/rs/

Rethinking Acceptable Use Policies to Enable Digital Learning: A Guide for School Districts: https://cosn.org/sites/default/files/pdf/Revised%20AUP%20March%202013_final.pdf

Webwise AUP Guidelines: https://www.webwise.ie/wp-content/uploads/2014/06/Webwise AUPGuidelines-1.pdf

Collaborative Tools

Google Docs: https://www.google.com/docs/about/

Google Slides: https://www.google.com/slides/about/

ePortfolio Tools (including Learning Management Systems)

Blackboard: http://www.blackboard.com/

Canvas: https://www.canvaslms.com/

Digication: https://www.digication.com/

Edublogs: https://edublogs.org/

Google Sites: https://sites.google.com/

Kidblog: https://kidblog.org/

Moodle: https://moodle.com/

PortfolioGen: https://www.portfoliogen.com/

Portfolium: https://portfolium.com/

SeeSaw: https://web.seesaw.me

Weebly: https://www.weebly.com/

Wix: https://www.wix.com/

Graphic Organizers

Bubbl.us: https://bubbl.us/

Inspiration: http://www.inspiration.com/

Kidspiration: http://www.inspiration.com/Kidspiration

MindMeister: https://www.mindmeister.com/

MindMup: https://app.mindmup.com/

Popplet: https://popplet.com/

SimpleMind+: (app available on iTunes)

Internet Resources to Support Student Writing

See Table 6.3.

Multimedia/Presentation Programs

PowerPoint: https://products.office.com/en-us/powerpoint

Powtoon: https://www.powtoon.com/

Screencastify: https://www.screencastify.com/

Screencast-O-Matic: https://screencast-o-matic.com/

Voki: http://www.voki.com

Online Library Resources

See Table 6.2.

Research and Writing Resources for Older Students

Google Scholar: https://scholar.google.com/

OWL Purdue Online Writing Lab: https://owl.english.purdue.edu/owl/

Resources for Teachers

ReadThinkWrite: http://www.readwritethink.org/

Rubric Maker: http://rubric-maker.com/

21st Century Skills Early Learning Framework and Guide: http://www.p21.org/our-work/elf

Web Content Accessibility Guidelines (WCAG): https://www.w3.org/WAI/intro/wcag

Search Engines Specifically Designed for Children

See Table 6.1.

REFERENCES

Agbayahoun, J. P. 2016. Teacher written feedback on student writing: Teachers' and learners' perspectives. *Theory and Practice in Language Studies*, 6(10), 1895–1904.

American Library Association. 2015. *Framework for Information Literacy for Higher Education* [online]. Available at: http://www.ala.org/acrl/standards/ilframework. Accessed on December 23, 2017.

Barron, A. E. and Ivers, K. S. 1998. *The internet and instruction: Activities and ideas* (2nd ed.). Englewood, CO: Libraries Unlimited.

Bernadowski, C. 2016. "I can't 'evn' get why she would make me 'rite' in her class:" Using think-alouds in middle school math for "at-risk" students. *Middle School Journal*, 47(4), 3–14.

Bostiga, S. E., Cantin, M. L., Fontana, C. V., and Casa, T. M. 2016. Moving math in the write direction. *Teaching Children Mathematics*, 22(9), 546–554.

Bradford, K., Newland, A., Rule, A., and Montgomery, S. 2016. Rubrics as a tool in writing instruction: Effects on the opinion essays of first and second graders. *Early Childhood Education Journal*, 44 (5), 463–472.

Brown, S. 2015 The impact of the ePortfolio tool on the process: Functional decisions of a new genre. *Theory into Practice*, 54(4), 335–342.

Buyarski, C. A., Aaron, R. W., Hansen, M. J., Hollingsworth, C. D., Johnson, C. A., Kahn, S., Landis, C. M., Pedersen, J. S., and Powell, A. A. 2015. Purpose and pedagogy: A conceptual model for an ePortfolio. *Theory into Practice*, 54(4), 283–291.

California Department of Education. 2015. California K–12 Education Technology Plan Template, Criteria, and Guiding Questions. Available at: https://www.cde.ca.gov/ls/et/rs/. Accessed on May 5, 2018.

Choi, M., Glassman, M., and Cristol, D. 2017. What it means to be a citizen in the internet age: Development of a reliable and valid digital citizenship scale. *Computers & Education*, 107, 100–112.

Clarke, L. and Abbott, L. 2016. Young pupils', their teacher's and classroom assistants' experiences of iPads in a Northern Ireland school: "Four and five years old, who would have thought they could do that?" *British Journal of Educational Technology*, 47(6), 1051–1064.

Common Core State Standards Initiative. 2017. English Language Arts Standards: Anchor Standards: College and Career Readiness Anchor Standards for Writing [online]. Available at: http://www.corestandards.org/ELA-Literacy/CCRA/W/. Accessed on December 30, 2017.

Common Sense Education. 2016. Scope & Sequence: Common Sense K–12 Digital Citizenship Curriculum [online]. Available at: https://www.commonsense.org/education/scope-and-sequence. Accessed on January 30, 2018.

Common Sense Media. n.d. What is digital citizenship? [video]. Available at: https://d1pmarobgdhgjx .cloudfront.net/education/WhatIsDigitalCitizenship_2017.mp4. Accessed on January 30, 2018.

Cooper, L. Z. 2014. Electronic portfolios to support the growth of digital identity in the school library. *School Libraries Worldwide*, *20*(2), 1–13.

Craig, R. and Blivin, J. 2016. Competency-based hiring: 10 signals the shift is happening. Available at: https://www.forbes.com/sites/ryancraig/2016/10/01/competency-based-hiring-10-signals-the -shift-is-happening/. Accessed on May 9, 2018.

Early, J. S. and Saidy, C. 2014. Uncovering substance: Teaching revision in high school classrooms. *Journal of Adolescent & Adult Literacy*, *58*(3), 209–218.

Federal Communications Commission. 2017. Children's Internet Protection Act (CIPA). Available at: https://www.fcc.gov/consumers/guides/childrens-internet-protection-act. Accessed on May 5, 2018.

Festa, K. 2017. The book trailer project: Media production within an integrated classroom. *Journal of Media Literacy Education*, *9*(2), 105–113.

Firmender, J. M., Casa, T. M., and Colonnese, M. W. 2017. Write on. *Teaching Children Mathematics*, *24*(2), 84–92.

Fisher, D. and Frey, N. 2013. A range of writing across the content areas. *Reading Teacher*, *67*(2), 96–101.

Fulton, L. 2017. Science notebooks as learning tools. *Science and Children*, *54*(6), 80–85.

Gerde, H. K., Foster, T. D., and Skibbe, L. E. 2014. Beyond the pencil: Expanding the occupational therapists' role in helping young children to develop writing skills. *Open Journal of Occupational Therapy*, *2*(1), 1–19.

Gielen, S., Peeters, E., Dochy, F., Onghena, P., and Struyven, K. 2010. Improving the effectiveness of peer feedback for learning. *Learning and Instruction*, *20*(4), 304–315.

Graham, S. and Harris, K. R. 2016. A path to better writing. *Reading Teacher*, *69*(4), 359–365.

Golden, J. C. and Jacoby, J. W. 2017. Playing princess: Preschool girls' interpretations of gender stereotypes in Disney Princess media. *Sex Roles*, *79*(5–6), 1–15.

Harrington, T. 2018. A focus on writing in every class is key to success in this rural California district. EdSource [online]. Available at: https://edsource.org/2018/a-focus-on-writing-in-every-class-is -key-to-success-in-this-rural-california-district/592228. Accessed on January 9, 2018.

Hart Research Associates. 2013. It takes more than a major: Employer priorities for college learning and student success. *Liberal Education*, *99*(2). Available at: https://www.aacu.org/publications -research/periodicals/it-takes-more-major-employer-priorities-college-learning-and. Accessed on May 5, 2018.

Hollandsworth, R., Donovan, J., and Welch, M. 2017. Digital citizenship: You can't go home again. *TechTrends: Linking Research and Practice to Improve Learning*, *61*(6), 524–530.

International Society for Technology in Education. 2016. ISTE Standards for Students [online]. Available at: https://www.iste.org/standards/standards-for-students. Accessed on August 18, 2018.

Isman, A. and Canan Gungoren, O. 2013. Being digital citizen. *Procedia—Social and Behavioral Sciences*, *106*, 551–556.

Ivers, K. S. 2003. *A teacher's guide to using technology in the classroom*. Westport, CT: Libraries Unlimited.

Ivers, K. S. and Barron, A. E. 2015. *Digital content creation in schools*. Santa Barbara, CA: ABC-CLIO.

Jones, L. M. and Mitchell, K. J. 2016. Defining and measuring youth digital citizenship. *New Media & Society, 18*(9), 2063–2079.

Koltay, T., Špiranec, S., and Karvalics, L. Z. 2015. The shift of information literacy towards Research 2.0. *Journal of Academic Librarianship, 41*(1), 87–93.

Kuh, G. D. 2008. *High-impact educational practices: What they are, who has access to them, and why they matter.* Washington, DC: Association of American Colleges & Universities.

Loretto, A., DeMartino, S., and Godley, A. 2016. Secondary students' perceptions of peer review of writing. *Research in the Teaching of English, 51*(2), 134–161.

MediaSmarts. n.d. Digital literacy fundamentals [online]. Available at: http://mediasmarts.ca/digital-media-literacy-fundamentals/digital-literacy-fundamentals. Accessed on April 21, 2018.

National Association for Media Literacy Education. 2007. Core Principles of Media Literacy Education in the United States [online]. Available at: https://drive.google.com/file/d/0B8j2T8jHrlgCYXVHSVJidWtmbmc/view. Accessed on April 21, 2018.

National Association for Media Literacy Education. 2014. Key questions to ask when analyzing media messages [online]. Available at: https://drive.google.com/file/d/0B8j2T8jHrlgCZ2Zta2hvWkF0dG8/view. Accessed on April 20, 2018.

Neuman, D. 2011. Constructing knowledge in the twenty-first century: I-LEARN and using information as a tool for learning. *School Library Research, 14*, 1–14. Available at: http://www.ala.org/aasl/sites/ala.org.aasl/files/content/aaslpubsandjournals/slr/vol14/SLR_ConstructingKnowledge_V14.pdf. Accessed on May 3, 2018.

Nicolaidou, I. 2013. E-portfolios supporting primary students' writing performance and peer feedback. *Computers & Education, 68*, 404–415.

Partnership for 21st Century Learning. 2007. *Framework for 21st Century Learning* [online]. Available at: http://www.p21.org/our-work/p21-framework. Accessed on September 18, 2017.

Partnership for 21st Century Learning. 2017. *21st Century Skills Early Learning Framework* [online]. Available at: http://www.p21.org/storage/documents/EarlyLearning_Framework/P21_ELF_Framework_Final.pdf. Accessed on April 21, 2018.

Ribble, M. 2014. Essential elements of digital citizenship. ISTE [online]. Available at: https://www.iste.org/explore/ArticleDetail?articleid=101. Accessed on January 30, 2018.

Spanke, J. and Paul, K. A. 2015. From the pens of babes: Authentic audiences for talented, young writers. *Gifted Child Today, 38*(3), 177–186.

Sperry, C. and Baker, F. 2016. Media literacy. *Social Education, 80*(3), 183–185.

Sullivan, C. 2016. Digital citizenship and the right to digital identity under international law. *Computer Law & Security Review, 32*, 474–481.

Šupšáková, B. 2016. Media education of children and youth as a path to media literacy. *Communication Today, 7*(1), 32–51.

Tecce DeCarlo, M., Grant, J., Lee, V. J., and Neuman, D. 2018. Information and digital literacies in a kindergarten classroom: An I-LEARN case study. *Early Childhood Education Journal, 46*(3), 265–275.

UNESCO. 2005. *Information and Communication Technologies in Schools: A Handbook for Teachers or How ICT Can Create New, Open Learning Environments.* Available at: http://unesdoc.unesco.org/images/0013/001390/139028e.pdf. Accessed on May 5, 2018.

Watson, C. E., Kuh, G. D., Rhodes, T., Light, T. P., and Chen, H. L. 2016. Editorial: ePortfolios—The eleventh high impact practice. *International Journal of ePortfolio*, 6(2), 65–69.

West, J. M. and Roberts, K. L. 2016. Caught up in curiosity: Genius hour in the kindergarten classroom. *Reading Teacher*, 70(2), 227–232.

Williams, M. G. and Korn, J. 2017. Othering and fear. *Journal of Communication Inquiry*, 41(1), 22–41.

Woo, M. M., Chu, S. K. W., and Li, X. 2013. Peer-feedback and revision process in a wiki mediated collaborative writing. *Educational Technology, Research and Development*, 61(2), 279–309.

World Wide Web Consortium. 2017. Web Content Accessibility Guidelines (WCAG) overview [online]. Available at: https://www.w3.org/WAI/intro/wcag. Accessed on April 20, 2018.

Website Evaluation Criteria Checklist

Topic of Research: _____   Grade Level:_____

Standard: _____

Site Name: _____   Last time the site was updated: _____

Site Purpose (check one):

__Business __Entertainment __Instructional __News __Personal __Political __Other _____

Website URL:_____

Criteria	Yes	No	N/A
Content			
Is the information being presented to influence? (e.g., Is bias present? Is it someone's opinion?)			
Explain:			
Is the information accurate? How do you know?			
Explain:			
Is the content free from typos and spelling, punctuation, and grammar errors?			
Is the site appropriate for its intended audience?			
Explain:			
Is the content free from advertisements?			
Is the author of the content listed?			
Is background or contact information available for the author?			
Layout and Design			
Is the layout clear? (consider organization, use of fonts, color, and images)			
Explain:			
Do the graphics, links, and other media support the information provided?			
Explain:			
Is it easy to navigate through the site?			
Explain:			
Recommendation			
Would you have your students use this website?			
Explain:			

Index

Accelerated Reader, 21, 22
Acceptable use policy (AUP), 141–42
Adobe Spark, 33, 50
Advanced research, 130–31
Agrin, D., 112
All About Me stories, 51, 135
American Association for the Advancement
    of Science (AAAS), 114
Antibullying resources, 67
Applied learning, 2
Arid Lands Information Network, 94
Armstrong, T., 54
Artificial intelligence (AI), 9
Aschbacher, P. R., 116
Asia Society, 88, 89
Association for Computing Machinery, 10
Association for Supervision and Curriculum
    Development (ASCD), 92
Association of American Colleges &
    Universities (AAC&U), 1, 3, 85, 143
Association of College & Research
    Libraries, 129
Asynchronous communication, 50
Augmented reality (AR), 93
Authority, and information literacy, 137

BaiBoard, 22
Baker, F., 140
Baker, R., 91
Barron, A. E., 32
Basic research, 130
Beaulieu-Jones, L., 19
Behfar, K., 26
Bias
    cultural, 53
    culturally responsive teachers
        and, 53
    implicit, 53, 60–61
    information literacy, 138
Bodily-kinesthetic intelligence, 54
Bolkan, S., 93
Book Creator, 33
Braille embossers, 66
BrckaLorenz, A., 22
Britt, L., 109
Brown, S., 143
Bruffee, K. A., 25
Bubbl.us, 113, 132, 134

Bureau of Educational and Cultural Affairs
    Exchange Programs, 99
Butler, T., 110

California Department of Education, 141
Career Readiness Anchor Standards for Writing,
    132–34
Cargile, A., 93
Center for Applied Special Technology, 60
Center for Global Education (Asia Society), 88
Center for Research on Education, Diversity,
    and Excellence (CREDE) Model, 19,
    21–22
Chapman-DeSousa, B., 21
Charter of the United Nations, 86
ChartGo program, 95
Chase, E., 63
Chen, H. L., 3
Children's Internet Protection Act (CIPA), 141
Cinderella, 86
Citizenship
    digital, 10, 144
    global, 88, 93
Clarke, E., 57
Climate Interactive, 96
Climate Time Machine, 96
Code.org, 10
Cognification, 9
Collaborative group learning, 31–34
College and Career Readiness Anchor Standards,
    130
Comer, D., 23
Common Core ELA/Literacy College,
    132–34
Common Sense Education, 144
Community Service Project Ideas for Students
    and Educators website, 113
Competency-based hiring, 143
Computer Aid International, 94
Computer literacy, defined, 10
Computer Science Teachers Association, 10
Conflict resolution, 91
Constructionism, 114, 119
Constructivist learning, 116
Constructivist teachers, 114
Cooperative group learning
    benefits and pitfalls of, 30–31
    technology and, 31–34

Cooperative learning, 22–34
   guidelines for facilitating face-to-face
         small group discourse, 24
   techniques, 26–30
   types of, 27
Cooperative learning group
   characteristics of, 25
   group processing, 25
   individual accountability, 25
   positive interdependence, 25
   promotive interaction, 25
   social skills, 25
Cooperative learning techniques, 26–30
   group investigation, 28
   Jigsaw method, 27
   learning together, 28
   Student Teams Achievement Divisions
         (STAD), 26
   Team-Assisted Individualization (TAI),
         26–27
   Teams Games Tournament (TGT), 26
Corbett, C., 61
Council of Chief State School Officers
      (CCSSO), 88
Crosspoint Antiracism website, 96
Cultural bias, 53
Cultural diversity, 49, 51, 88, 91, 93
Culturally responsive teachers, 52–53
Culturally responsive teaching, 51–59, 64, 68–69
   defined, 52
   overview, 49
   technology and, 55–57
Culture
   digital-age learning, 10
   high-context, 50
   low-context, 50
   resources for learning about different, 58
Curran, M., 53
Currency, and information literacy, 138
Cyberbullying, 66, 144
Cyber Innovation Center, 10

DDD-E (Decide, Design, Develop, and Evaluate)
      model, 32–35, 116
Delaplane, E., 110
DeNora, T., 57
Designing
   collaborative activities, 23, 32
   small group instruction, 19–22
Dewey, John, 109, 114
Digication, 142
Digital citizen, 144

Digital citizenship, 10
   categories for teaching, 144
   defined, 144
Digital content creation
   cognitive learning theories' relationships to,
         117–18
   constructivist components and their
         relationships to, 116
Digital Content Creation in Schools (Ivers and
      Barron), 32
Digital intelligence, 54
Digital literacy education, 144
Digital technologies, 93
Disney Princess media, 63, 140
Display or magnification software, 66
Diversity, 49, 111
   as component of global learning, 88
   cultural, 49, 51, 88, 91, 93
Domain extensions, 136–37
Domain name, 136
Donovan, J., 144
Duncan, A., 86
Dweck, C. S., 54–55

Edmodo, 33, 51, 113
Edublogs, 142
Education
   equitable, 60–68
   inclusive, 60–68
   just, 60–68
Educreations Interactive Whiteboard, 22
Environmental Protection Agency (EPA), 113
ePortfolios, 142–43, 145
   assessment of, 143
   guidelines for assigning and developing,
         143
   paper-based portfolios and, 142–43
Equitable classrooms, 64–68
Equitable education, 60–68
Evernote, 22, 33, 113

Facebook Messenger, 93
FaceTime (Apple), 93
Fair, C. D., 110
Festa, K., 135
Field Trip Earth, 97
Food pyramids, 96–97
Framework for 21st Century Learning, 1, 3–6,
      7–8, 142
*Framework for Developing Global and Cultural
      Competencies to Advance Equity, Excellence
      and Economic Competitiveness,* 92

Framework for State Action on Global Education, 88–89
Free-rider effect, 31

Gardner, Howard, 49, 53–55
Garvey, J. C., 22
Gay, G., 51–52
Gender-creative children, 63
Gender norms, 61
Global citizens, 93
Global citizenship, 88, 93
Global competence, 85–100
    defined, 88
    global learning and, 92–93
    overview, 85
    resources for teaching, 99
    skills associated with, 85
    supporting, 88–92
    technology supporting, 93–100
    working together, 86–88
Global Education 2030 Agenda, 86
Globalisation, as component of global learning, 91
Global learning, 8–9
    essential elements and strategies for implementing, 90
    global competence and, 92–93
    projects resources, 94–95
Global Lives Project, 57
Globally Competent Learning Continuum (GCLC), 92
Global Perspectives: A Framework for Global Education in Australian Schools (Rae, Baker and McNicol), 91
GoConqr's Mind Maps, 113
God Grew Tired of Us, 57
Golden, J. C., 63
Google Docs, 33, 98, 113, 132, 134
Google Expeditions, 97–98
Google Hangouts, 93
Google Keep, 22
Google Scholar, 132
Google Sites, 33, 142
Google Slides, 33, 132, 134
Graham, J. A., 110
"G Suite of Education," 134

Han, H., 50
Herman, J. L., 116
High-context cultures, 50
High-impact educational practices

Framework for 21st Century Learning, 3–6, 7–8
    integrative and applied learning, 2
    intellectual and practical skills, 2
    knowledge of human cultures, 2
    knowledge of physical and natural world, 2
    outcomes and, 1–3
    overview, 1
    personal and social responsibility, 2
    preparing students for future, 9
    technology, 6–9
Hill, C., 61
HIP technology, 1, 6–9
    preparing students for future, 9
    standards and frameworks, 9–11
Hollandsworth, R., 144
Human cultures, knowledge of, 2
Human rights, 91, 96
Hurtado, S. S., 22
Hypertext Transfer Protocol (HTTP), 136

Identity, as component of global learning, 91
I-LEARN model, 131–32
Implicit biases, 53, 60–61. *See also* Bias
Inclusive classrooms
    overview, 49
    technology and, 64–68
Inclusive education, 60–68
Industrial Revolution, 142
The Inevitable (Kelly), 9
Informal cooperative learning, 28–29
    Peer Instruction, 28
    Random Reporter, 29
    Think-Pair-Share, 28
    Whole Class Jigsaw, 28
Information, verification of, 138
Information and communication technologies (ICT) literacy, 140–42
Information literacy, 129, 136–38
    authority, 137
    bias, 138
    currency, 138
    domain name, 136
    layout, 137
    reason, 136
    target audience, 137
    verification of information, 138
Inspiration, 33, 113, 134
Integrative learning, 2

Intellectual skills, 1–2
Intelligence
    artificial, 9
    bodily-kinesthetic, 54
    defined, 53
    digital, 54
    interpersonal, 54
    intrapersonal, 54
    linguistic, 53
    logical-mathematical, 53
    multiple, 53–55
    musical, 54
    naturalist, 54
    pedagogical, 54
    spatial, 54
Interdependence, as component of global
        learning, 91
International Society for Technology in Education
        (ISTE), 6, 9–10, 85
Interpersonal intelligence, 54
Intrapersonal intelligence, 54
Ivers, K. S., 32

Jacoby, J.W., 63
Jigsaw method, 27
Johnson, D.W., 25–26, 85
Johnson R. T., 25–26, 85
Jones, L. M., 144
Just classrooms, 64–68
Just education, 60–68

K–12 Computer Science Framework,
        9–11
*K–12 Service-Learning Project Planning
        Toolkit,* 111
Karvalics, L. Z., 132
Katzarska-Miller, I., 93
Kelly, K., 1, 6, 9
Kelso, T., 63
Keynote, 33
Kidblog, 55, 142
Kidspiration, 33, 113, 134
Kid World Citizen, 85
Kilpatrick, W. H., 114
Knowledge
    of human cultures, 2
    of physical and natural world, 2
    work, 141
Kohr, R., 110–11
Koltay, T., 132
Koskey, K. L. K., 31

Koutamanis, M., 50
Kuh, G. D., 3, 5, 6
Kuster, M., 23

Language resources, 98
Latopolski, K., 22
Layout, and information literacy, 137
Learn and Serve America, 111
Learning
    applied, 2
    cooperative, 22–34
    integrative, 2
    project-based, 113–19
    service, 109–13
Lee, H., 31
Lenaghan, J., 23
LGBTQ+ individuals, 61–66, 96, 139
Liberal Education and America's Promise
        (LEAP) initiative, 1, 5
Light, T. P., 3
Lim, C., 31
Linguistic intelligence, 53
Linnenbrink-Garcia, 31
Literacy
    ICT, 140–42
    information, 136–38
    media, 139–40
Little Red Riding Hood, 86
Logical-mathematical intelligence, 53
Low-context cultures, 50

Maarifa Centres, 94
Mandela, Nelson, 61
Mannix, E., 26
Math Is Fun: Make Your Own Graphs program,
        95
McNicol, C., 91
Media
    children and, 63
    LGBTQ+ individuals and, 62–63
    perpetuating stereotypes, 62–64
    portrayal of people in poverty, 63
    poverty and, 63
Media literacy, 139–40
Microsoft Education, 97
Microsoft Innovative Educator, 97
Mindcraft economy, 141
MindMeister, 33, 113, 134
MindMup, 33, 113, 134
Mitchell, K. J., 144
Moodle, 33, 51, 113, 143

Multiple intelligence, 53–55
  resources for assessing, 57
  roles in digital content creation, 56
Musical intelligence, 54

Nam, C.W., 29
National Association for Media Literacy
    Education, 139
National Center on Universal Design for
    Learning, 60
National Council for the Social Studies
    (NCSS), 114
National Council of Teachers of Mathematics
    (NCTM), 114
National Geographic, 57
National Math and Science Initiative, 10
National Service-Learning Clearinghouse, 111
National Youth Leadership Council, 113
Naturalist intelligence, 54
NCES (National Center for Education Statistics)
    Kid's Zone Create a Graph site, 95
Neuman, D., 131

Online communication, 50
Online library resources, 133
Organisation for Economic Co-Operation and
    Development (OECD), 23
Original research, 131–32
OWL Purdue Online Writing Lab, 132

Paper-based portfolios, 142–43
Partnership for 21st Century Learning (P21), 3, 5,
    85, 142
Peace building, as component of global learning, 91
Pedagogical intelligence, 54
Peter, J., 50
Peterson, R., 26
Piaget, Jean, 114
Pinterest, 113
Popplet, 33, 113, 132, 134
PortfolioGen, 55, 142
Poverty, and media, 63
PowerPoint, 33, 134
Powtoon, 134
Practical skills, 2
Prezi, 33
Proctor, C., 19
Progressive education movement, 109
Project-based learning, 113–19
  overview, 109
  resources for, 118
  technology supporting, 115–19

Project Foundry, 33, 113
Protecting Children in the 21st Century Act,
    141

Racial discrimination, 61
Rae, L., 91
ReadThinkWrite, 134
Reason, and information literacy, 136
Reed, P., 110
Research, 129–32
  advanced, 130–31
  basic, 130
  original, 131–32
  technology supporting, 132
Research as Inquiry, 129–30
Research to Build and Present Knowledge,
    130
Reysen, S., 93
Rhodes, T., 3
Ribble, M., 144
RMC Research Corporation, 111
Rockwood, H. S., III, 25
Rogat, T. K., 31
Rose, A., 61
Rubric Maker, 134

Scott, K. E., 110
Screencastify, 51, 134
Screencast-O-Matic, 51, 134
Screen readers, 66
Search engines, 131
SeeSaw digital portfolio system, 142
Service-learning, 8–9, 109–13
  civic values and critical citizenship,
      109–10
  overview, 109
  skill-set practice and reflexivity, 109–10
  social justice activism, 109–10
  technology supporting, 112–13
Service-learning projects, 110–11
Shadow Puppet Edu, 33
ShowMe, 22, 50
Simons, P. R. J., 116
SimpleMind+, 33, 113, 134
Skills
  intellectual, 1–2
  practical, 1–2
Skype, 22, 93, 97, 113
Slavin, R. E., 28
Small group instruction
  CREDE Professional Development Model,
      21–22

designing, 19–22
guidelines for creating small, instructional groups, 20
managing, 19–22
technology and, 22
Social competence, 49–51
defined, 49
overview, 49
technology and, 50–51
Social justice, as component of global learning, 91
Social loafing, 31
Social media, 1, 50, 97, 113, 140
Social movements, 61
Social success, defined, 63
Spatial intelligence, 54
Speech/voice recognition software, 66
Sperry, C., 140
Spiranec, S., 132
STEAM (science, technology, engineering, art, and mathematics), 110
STEM (science, technology, engineering, and mathematics), 1, 49, 61, 97, 110
Stereotypes, and media, 62–64
ST (JiJi) Math, 21, 22
Students
with disabilities, 67
high-impact educational practices and, 9
research, and technology, 132
writing, internet resources to support, 135
Student Teams Achievement Divisions (STAD), 26
Sucker effect, 31
SurveyMonkey, 55
SurveyPlanet, 55
Sustainable Development Goal 4, 86

Target audience, and information literacy, 137
Teachers
evaluation of, 92
resources that help teachers connect with other, 52
Team-Assisted Individualization (TAI), 26–27
Teams Games Tournament (TGT), 26
Technology
collaborative and cooperative group learning and, 31–34
culturally responsive teaching and, 55–57
donations and grants resources, 68
global competence and, 93–100
HIP, 1, 6–11

just, equitable, and inclusive classrooms and, 64–68
project-based learning and, 115–19
research and, 132
small group instruction and, 22
social competence and, 50–51
student research and, 132
writing and, 134–35
Text-to-speech programs, 66
The Advocates for Human Rights website, 96
The Lost Boys, 57
Theory of Multiple Intelligences, 49, 53–55
Think Global, 88
Thomas, M., 50
Tomasello, M., 8
Tomlinson-Clarke, S., 53
Translation websites and apps, 59
Trochim, W., 26

UCAR (University Corporation for Atmospheric Research) Center for Science, 96
UN Educational, Scientific and Cultural Organization (UNESCO), 86, 141
United Nations, 86, 88
Agenda for Sustainable Development, 86
Sustainable Development Goal 4, 86, 88
Sustainable Development Goals, 86–87
Universal Declaration of Human Rights Article 26, 110
Universal Design for Learning (UDL)
curriculum, 60
assessment, 60
goals, 60
materials, 60
methods, 60
University of Minnesota, 29
U.S. Department of Education, 92
U.S. News and World Report, 112

Valkenburg, P. M., 50
Verification of information, 138
Videoconferencing, 113
Virtual field trips, 93
Virtual reality (VR), 9
VoiceThread, 22, 51
Voki, 134–35
Vossen, H. G. M., 50
Vuoskoski, J., 57
Vygotsky, L. S., 114

Walker, A. B., 111
Walker, R., 63
Wasik, B., 20
Watson, C. E., 3
Web 2.0 technologies, 93, 132
Web Content Accessibility Guidelines
        (WCAG), 138
Weebly, 33, 55, 142
Weinstein, C., 53
Welch, M., 144
What Do We Do All Day site, 85
Winters, L., 116

Wix, 33, 142
Wohl, A., 62
Word prediction software, 66
World Wide Web Consortium
        (W3C), 138
Writing, 132–35
Wyatt, T., 21

YouTube, 54

Zoom, 22, 51, 93, 113
ZubaBoxes, 94

About the Author

KAREN S. IVERS is a professor at California State University, Fullerton. She has published multiple books and numerous articles on educational technology. Her awards include Distinguished Faculty Marshall; Teaching and Technology Innovations; Honor an Educator; and Outstanding Faculty Recognition for Service, Scholarship, and Creativity.